D1418627

COME FLY WITH THE BUTTERFLY

Come Fly With The Butterfly

THE TEN SECRETS OF SUCCESSFUL PUNTING

JOHN MORT GREEN

Edited by MICHAEL LITCHFIELD

PELHAM BOOKS

First published in Great Britain by
PELHAM BOOKS LTD
26 Bloomsbury Street
London, W.C.1
1969

© 1969 *by John Mort Green and Michael Litchfield*

7207 0276 3

Set and printed in Great Britain by Tonbridge Printers Ltd, Peach Hall Works, Tonbridge, Kent, in Garamond twelve on thirteen point, and bound by James Burn at Esher, Surrey

I should like to thank Michael Litchfield for writing and compiling this book for me. I want also to thank all bookmakers because if it were not for them and their money I should have no story to tell.

JOHN MORT GREEN

CONTENTS

ILLUSTRATIONS

Introduction

Thrifty old aunts and penniless uncles will warn you: 'There is only one winner in horse racing - the bookmaker.'

My advice to you is block your ears with their old lace and take notice of me - John Mort Green, a professional punter with good looks and good sense and a damned good bank balance.

The 'wise' aunt has probably lost her knickers at bingo and the uncle has been kicking stones about for a few days after blowing his wages in the betting shop. And they don't want you to gamble because they want to 'tap' you for a few quid!

Why should you listen to me? I'll give you one good reason; for the sake of money. Can you think of a better reason? If you can, then don't read on because punting for profit is strictly not for you.

I am one of a handful of people who make a lucrative, tax-free living out of racing in Britain consistently every year. I make £200 a week, at least, every year. That is my salary, an enviable income paid wholly, although not always with a smile, by the bookmakers.

Every professional punter soon discovers that he has been christened with a nickname, which sticks with him for the rest of his racing days. For example, there is Under the Bed Stevie, Snowey Bill, Tell a Lie Jerry, Silent Jim Brighton, Good Book Joe, The Blonde Viking God, Long Larry and Mickey Fingers. I am known as Soupbones in my homeland, Australia, because I am so slim, and as The Butterfly in Britain. I may flutter about like a butterfly gone berserk on the racecourse, but when it comes to betting I sting like a bee. You can ask any of the big bookmakers for confirmation of that.

Jealous people usually call me a lay-about. My friends call me a lay-about, except they say it with a smile. Name me another lay-about who makes a conservative £200 tax-free a week on top of expenses, without breaking the law? And those expenses include a vivacious blonde-haired chauffeur to drive me by Rolls-Royce to British racecourses and a private plane to fly me to the French tracks at week-ends.

At my luxury flat in London's West End, I have a wardrobe of suits, each one costing a hundred guineas, and all of them paid for me by the bookies.

Please do not forget the ladies in my life, either. They also have to come out of expenses. Yes, they have to be made-to-measure, too. Nothing must be off-the-peg for The Butterfly. Only the best, and I reckon myself an expert judge of any filly, whether it has two or four legs.

Newspaper columnists have labelled me a playboy. How right they are! Boy, I play real hard with the ladies when the day's business is done. Remember, though, work and women is a deadly cocktail. They just do not mix. That is number one rule the professional punter must learn.

The London Hilton Hotel, the West End casinos and night clubs are my favourite stamping grounds when I want to impress people, such as wealthy girl-friends, or not so rich females who make up for their cash deficiencies with certain other assets!

In this trade it is essential to keep on impressing

people. If you walk and talk big, then you become big. The only people with inferiority complexes are inferior people. I have never married because my philosophy is that every day should be a honeymoon. In some countries I have been written up as a joke. I must be one of the richest clowns in the world!

My background has given me a few furlongs start on anybody else in the satisfying profession of relieving affluent bookmakers of their money made from mugs. My father was a bookmaker and I followed in his footsteps. So I learned all the mistakes of the punter from the safer side of the fence. But in these days of the betting tax, I know where the grass is greener, providing you know your trade; just like a draughts-man, you must know where to draw the line! The successful punter has the steel nerves of James Bond, the temperament of a robot and the confidence of John Mort Green.

I also became a trainer and rode in trotting races so that I was familiar with every facet of the racing industry. To become a punting tycoon you must be an expert on every aspect of the business. Most people do not have the opportunity that I had to achieve such direct contact with all the different spheres of racing, so they must become armchair students.

When I first came to Britain, the bookmakers thought that I was a pantomime. They saw me flitting around on my toes all over the ring in coloured hats and thought that I was just a big, skinny comic, not to be taken seriously at all. At first they treated me with absolute contempt. I was just a mug Aussie Oswald, a ya-hoo they would reduce to poverty in no time at all. After paying me £5,000, then £2,000 another day, they began to think the strange creature from the Antipodes should be taken seriously after all.

At the racecourse I wear a single red glove without fingers so that I am easily recognisable by bookies in the ring. I have never done a real hard day's work in my life, but I can tell you if any horse has been having bad dreams. I have no incentive to be a millionaire, I want only to live like one. You, too, can enjoy the sweet life – if you are prepared to accept my advice and conform with my Ten Commandments. They are:

1. Thou shalt not be greedy.
2. Thou shalt back only good horses, ridden by top jockeys and trained by the most famous trainers.
3. Thou must forget those 20-1 outsiders. The majority of winners start at between evens and 5-1, and it is within this price range that one should look for the best bets.
4. When ye have got your winner, go home early if you are at the races or in the betting shop; do anything, get drunk, beat the wife, start collecting milk bottle tops, but do not have another bet that day.
5. Ye must always back unfashionable jockeys on the Tote. This is because most people who invest on the Tote are amateur punters who follow the Piggotts, Hutchinsons, Lindleys and Mercers, even if they are riding camels with the humps on their feet. To back an unfashionable rider is not breaking the second commandment. Bill Williamson, for example, would not top any popularity poll among the public, and yet he is one of the greatest judges of pace in racing today.
6. Thou must always watch for significant jockey changes from the declarations in the morning newspapers.
7. Thee must know the heavy-betting stables and wait and watch for their cash to go down.

8. Ye must always try to understand the workings of the minds of trainers and jockeys, both straight and crooked.

9. Ye must be firm about getting good value; an odds-on chance rarely represents good value, and treat such bets with maximum caution.

10. Remember, remember, if you lose £100 all you've lost are ten little pieces of paper with ones and naughts on them, but lose your confidence and you have lost everything.

I have talked about myself at some length, not only because I find it an interesting subject, but also so that you can appreciate the kind of make-up necessary for a man to become a successful professional punter.

I am friendly with most of the Australian jockeys in Britain. Many people, including racecourse officials and the Press, have suggested that the Aussie boys are telling me when they are going to win. They are wrong. The truth, in fact, is the opposite. I could tell *them* when they are going to win. You see, I have to be a walking racing encyclopaedia. I must know the Form Book like an actor has to learn a script. But very few jockeys are good judges of horses. So they come to me to find out when they are going to score. However, my opinion of most jockeys is that they are over-grown midgets who have become glorified choir boys, but more about them later.

Certain races, such as the supporting events on Derby Day, should be left alone by anyone who does not want to contribute to the Bookmakers' Winter Sunshine Holiday Fund. Talking of Derby Day, in 1964 I didn't believe in Santa Claus. In 1965 I took the wrong price at one stage about Sea Bird and the following year some clown dropped a jellied eel down the inside front of my Moss Bros pin-stripes. Further-

more, the jellied eel was alive. The only way to go to
Epsom on Derby Day is reclining in the back of a
Rolls Royce, driven by a beautiful blonde woman
chauffeur, with a basket of Dom Perignon '59 and
chicken sandwiches in the boot, and some witty
friends in the front seat to provide the amusing chat.
I do not think that I could stomach the Derby any
other way.

It's a really terrible day for a professional punter.
Too many things can happen to distract the concentra-
tion. Upsetting things like a skinny, yellow-toothed
gipsy jumping from behind a bush, wanting five bob
to stick a sprig of stinking heather on your lapel and
then, while pinning it on with the left hand, the right
hand is slipping inside your jacket to the wallet. What
a shocking, ghastly thing to do to an honest, non-tax
paying professional punter!

I'll give you a good tip for the Derby – get yourself
a nice box in the grandstand, get sloshed on champagne
all day and don't worry a snap about the horses. This
is what the smarties do. They climb up to the rarefied
atmosphere on top of that giant grandstand and they
are eating and drinking all day long. They would not
even know that the horses are running around.

Me, I bet on the four-legged, ugly things down
below and I have to be around close to them to see
what is going on. I see the races by buying a wooden
Coca Cola box from the barman at the nearest bar. A
couple of minutes before each race he hands it over to
me. Then I stand on it somewhere near the bookmakers
on the rails and I'm a foot above everyone else so that
I can see everything.

So take my tip and spend five shillings on a Coca
Cola box. They are half an inch thicker than the
Schweppes bitter lemon boxes.

The thing that I hate about the Derby is that it's so stiff and formal. On Derby Day, more than any other day, if you are watching from the Members' Enclosure, it is essential to take very restricting control over your emotions.

If you've had your last ten quid on a 100-1 outsider and it has got up in a photograph finish, it's not considered polite to jump eight feet in the air and yell out, 'Whoooppeeeee! You bloody beauteeeeeeeee!' What you are supposed to do is nod your head approvingly, clap your hands four times, and say, almost under your breath, 'Oh, well done jockey Lindley,' or something like that. It's very restricting, but I've seen members who would rather die than show their emotions on a racecourse. They do die sometimes.

Their horse has just got up from nowhere to win the Ascot Gold Cup by a nose or something and the bloated-bellied old boy in the morning suit, who owns it, doesn't say a word. He just goes black in the face, his eyes pop out and he keels over stone dead. With his dying breath he says, 'Well done, Lester.' See what I mean? At Epsom on Derby Day, you must control yourself, even if it kills you.

Now a word about Derby Day drinking. My advice to you is go for your life, get yourself cock-eyed. On Derby Day you are better off getting stoned than betting, considering some of the reptiles that manage to get up and win on classic days like that. The trouble is that the bars are always so crowded. Someone like Lord Cockwirthy-Pugh, the internationally-known two-pint paraplegic, will be impossible to avoid. He will bump into you, spilling eight gallons of Charringtons all over your latest Savile Row sensation.

Personally, when I go to Epsom on Derby Day, I take my own bar with me. It is all in the boot of my

Rolls-Royce, guarded even more than her virtue by my chauffeur. Between the second race and the Derby, there is always an interval of an hour and that is the time to hotfoot it around to the car park and slosh it down, eating the sandwiches, too, with my little finger extended to impress any aristocracy passing by. Appearances are everything, my mother always told me.

Don't, don't, don't go to the Derby in something gauche like a Miami blue suit, with a gas chamber green, snap brim Madison Avenue hat and imitation yellow, snakeskin leather shoes. I did once. The barman charged me an extra thirty bob for the hire of the Coca Cola box.

CHAPTER ONE

The Social Circuit

The Butterfly may not be too well up on his Latin, but his family has a motto which, when translated, goes something roughly like, 'A winner a day keeps the bailiff away.' It may not have the polish of those tonsil-tangling words in some heraldic crests, but I can promise you that it is more profitable.

Some people – usually amateur head-shrinkers who try to examine me like the gas man reading a meter and probably hoping that in some deep, hidden cavity of my fantastic, beautiful brain he will discover the secret to tomorrow's 2.30 race – ask me what I want out of life. The serious answer is, I do not know. I do know that I do not want to be an empire builder. When I am dead I have no desire for a statue to be built in remembrance of me, with people laying wreaths around my stone feet every Sunday. I do not want to go on the stage, so that rules out the theatre, films, television and Parliament. If I became a doctor I would turn into a hypochondriac and crowd out my own waiting room. All I wish is to have sufficient money to be able to do what I want when I have discovered what that is, if you see what I mean. It may transpire that I develop a compulsion to become a sticker of sticks in ice lollipops. In which case, I shall have enough money to buy more sticks than anyone else in the same chilly business.

In many ways, racing is just like any other trade. In

other words, it is often more important who you know rather than what you know. The professional punter must ease himself into the right circles. He does not have to like the people. All he has to do is live with them!

It was while doing the social circuit early in 1968 that I heard for certain that 'Scobie' Breasley, the grandpop jockey, was going to retire at the end of the season. This sort of snippet of information is very important. After all, no man is going to ride himself to death and risk slipping a golden disc when on the threshold of retirement by rushing all over the globe for mounts. In other words, he would be riding only well-fancied runners outside his own stable. Sure enough, Breasley retired at the end of the 1968 season to take up training at the late Walter Nightingall's yard at Epsom.

All these amazing bits of information come from unbelievable Mayfair parties the English aristocracy throw some nights because it happens to be Beethoven's birthday, or some other world-shattering anniversary like that. At dings like those you can find out anything.

All these barons and earls and marchionesses and countesses and duchesses are sitting around, carving their initials in the Queen Anne furniture, all stoned out of their tiny minds with their diamonds dangling in their cocktails and that is when they start telling their little secrets. As the Butterfly flits around the room titillating Countess Flossie with his fund of Queensland sheep-shearing jokes, he hears sensational little snippets like, '*She's* going to be giving it to *him* this year.' Ecstasy! What a scoop! Interpreted, of course, to mean that the subject of the gossip, whomever he might be, is going to be very much in the news and receive countless congratulations from a wide circle of friends shortly.

The important point is that racing's inner sanctum knew about Breasley's plans well in advance. There is a certain coterie of aristocratic racing people in Britain who can even tell you what the Queen is having for breakfast next Pancake Tuesday. Everyone in the social circus was talking about 'Scobie's' future. All the signs were there that he would take up training when he retired from the saddle. He had enjoyed a fabulous career, winning five Caulfield Cups and two English Derbies. He had never been in serious trouble as a rider with English stewards and he had made a fortune beyond the wildest dreams of most jockeys. You should have seen his place at Putney before he moved down to Epsom. It was an enormous Spanish-styled mansion that must have cost him a quarter of a million dollars at least, and he had a bigger staff of Chinese helps that at the Nan King café. What a luxury life he leads. His chauffeur drives him to the races in a twenty-feet long Rolls-Royce with the number plate SB fifty-something–whatever his current age happens to be. Isn't he a one?

'Scobie' made a satisfactory start to his new career, saddling a winner early in his first season as a trainer. His debut in the winner's enclosure as a trainer came at Lingfield Park (known as 'Leafy Lingfield' because of its picturesque setting) on May 17, 1969. The horse which won him the right to be there was Benroy, ridden by Frankie Durr, the handicap specialist. Benroy started 3–1 favourite for the Four Elms Handicap Sweepstakes for three-year-olds and up-wards, run over one mile and two furlongs. Frankie utilised all his old dash to drive Benroy well clear.

'Scobie' sits back in his big Rolls luxuriating in the

ecstasy of it all. He is so tiny and he sits so low in the seat that you can barely see the top of his hat through the back window. 'Scobie' always wears a hat. He is going a bit bald these days and he has acquired a psychological thing about it. You would have to creep up behind him with the London Symphony Orchestra playing 'God Save the Queen' to get him to take it off.

Breasley always spends the British winter in Barbados. But even that far away he keeps well in touch with the English racing scene. When he went water ski-ing while a jockey, he would arrange for a telephone to be taken right out to the pier where the speedboat tied up, in case an English trainer rang him up to engage him for a ride in one of the big races of the new season.

'Scobie' was lying on a beach in Barbados in January, 1964, when he was booked to partner Santa Claus, the eventual English Derby winner some five months later. 'Scobie' is crazy about Barbados. He has got a permanent luxury home there, built to his own design and no doubt this is the place to which he will retire completely when even he is too senile to get a leg across the back of a horse. Now that he has turned to training, even more he will be able to eat good food, lie in the sun and water ski. And, boy, can he water ski! He is one of the best, and with his astonishing physical strength he can keep at it all day long while other younger jockeys who visit him, like Australia's Ron Hutchinson, are lying flat out exhausted on the beach, yelling at the silly old man to quit before he has a coronary or a hernia or something serious. But 'Scobie' laughs at them. He knows that he is a superman.

Jockeys in Britain have always stood in awe of

'Scobie', more so than for any other rider in the world, including Lester Piggott. They are always begging Breasley to join their little golfing groups, always inviting him to dinner, always trying to get in good with him. Among jockeys, he was a king, and also among the upper-crust racehorse owners.

'By jove!' would exclaim some of those barrel-bellied old boys with their seventy-eight hyphened names when 'Scobie's' genius got a winner. 'By jove, by jove, by jove,' they said, 'wasn't that an absolutely wizard ride, what?' This was said because those kind of bluebloods admired the subtleties of 'Scobie's' style. He came flying across the line, sometimes sitting as still as a statue. But Lester Piggott, tut, tut, that is a very different story. Many racing people think that Lester would cut a horse in two to reach the wire first, but this could not be further from the truth. They love Lester in Tattersall's, but not so much in the Members' Enclosure, where it is considered by many as 'just not on'. Although he is no butcher, Piggott will never, in my opinion, reach the status of 'Scobie' in the eyes of the racing bluebloods in Britain.

'Scobie' has become the most popular figure in British racing. When he had a fall at Newbury eight weeks before the end of one season, it was like a war-time disaster; 'The *Hood's* gone down', something like that. Racing men all over the country rang the hospital to see if the old maestro was all right.

Racing folk are not renowned for their loyalty. With 'Scobie' it was different. Among the general racing public he was hero-worshipped. Every time he lost another hair his fans wept.

Early in 1967 a Derby colt was waiting in a white wooden classic box at Newmarket for a skinny, long-nosed, temperamental, half-bald, superhuman little jockey from Sydney. The colt was Royal Palace. The jockey was George 'Cottonfingers' Moore, and when they got together it was the greatest love affair since Batman and Robin. They made history together and for the three of us it was one of the greatest Derbies since the mutations that changed the apes into bookmakers.

It was because of Derby Day and this fantastic colt, Royal Palace, that George decided to give up his regular treble a week at Randwick and take that 12,000 mile trip to Britain. Money had nothing to do with it. What is money to a man like George Moore, apart from food, clothing and a place to sleep? George came to England for one reason, and that was to win the English Derby.

Noel Murless, the trainer he rode for, no doubt was on that hot line to Sydney week after week telling George all about the practically unbeatable certainty he had all wound up for the big one at Epsom. He must have told George how sensationally Royal Palace, with Piggott up, won the Royal Lodge Stakes at Ascot, the first classic mile race for two-year-olds the previous season.

The colt was left six lengths at the start and yet this super son of Ballymoss strolled home a length and a half in front, after easily catching and joining the best baby thoroughbreds in the land at the two-furlong post. It was the best Derby trial by any two-year-old of the season and Lester Piggott, the Murless stable jockey, was looking set to collect his fourth Derby.

The Piggott-Murless partnership seemed to be as secure as a Victorian marriage. Then one bright morning Lester announced a separation, just like that, creating what could be termed a sensation, even by George Moore's standards. That is why the real

George Moore came to England to ride for Noel Murless.

The thing is that when George arrived in Britain he had to forget that he was George Moore. He had to act like all the nice, sweet, well-mannered little fellows that they call jockeys in Britain and that meant, when he was in the saddling enclosure, he had to behave like every other jockey. First of all, he learned to salute the owner and then take one step back, not speaking a word until spoken to. Noel Murless is no more democratic than any other English trainer. He was brought up to believe that in British racing the owner is top, the trainer second and the jockey tolerated.

But with so much at stake, George played the scene very cool. He had been here before and he knew the score. Riding for the late Aly Khan in the 1959 and 1960 seasons, he won some of the biggest races in France and England – races like the Grand Prix de Paris, the Ascot Gold Cup, the Sussex Stakes and the Ebor Handicap. George had a ball then. It was win, win all day and celebrations all night.

Aly Khan took a great liking to his little jockey and he introduced George to all the big shots in French and English society, taking him to some of those high-rolling jet set parties. For George then it was champagne, caviar and Folies Bergères all the way. A fantasy time, the last days of Rome stuff.

Then came the car crash. Aly was kaput and socially so was George. With no Aly around, George was just another jockey again to the snooty international set. So George went home with his beautiful wife, Iris, to Sydney where a jockey has the social standing somewhere between a brain surgeon and a Supreme Court judge.

After seven years, and with less hair on top, but with

more racing talent than ever he had, George came back to England. He still had a ball, occasionally, with his racing friends taking him around the West End nightspots, but there was no one around London quite like the original swinger, Aly Khan, except maybe me.

On this occasion, George did not come for fun. He came for Royal Palace. Two and a half months before the Derby, Royal Palace was equal favourite with Ribocco, a nuggety bay colt to be ridden by Lester Piggott. But 'The Palace' was the cat I was nuts about. So was his owner, the multi-millionaire racing man, Mr H. Joel. When Piggott left Murless, Mr Joel's poor heart suddenly went thump-plonk-trippety. He saw his life's dream of winning a Derby slipping away from him like the third ace in a poker machine. Most Derbies are won by only the great jockeys. So, with Piggott gone, Mr Joel was in big heaps of trouble.

'I don't care if you search the whole world,' was, I imagine, the gist of what he said to Murless, 'but get me the greatest jockey there is!' Money was no object. Mr Joel has several rooms full of the stuff. The rumour is that George said a flat 'no' when he was first asked to come, but the retainer price must have kept going up and up, because it took him six weeks to say 'yes, I'll come,' probably for the highest retainer ever given to a foreign jockey to ride in Britain.

I defended George in an argument once after a meeting at Moonee Valley a few years ago when he had been beaten on three hot favourites. As I recall, I hadn't backed any of them. Anyway, a Melbourne bookmaker said George was not worth anything away from Sydney tracks and he was especially spastic around little tricky tracks like Moonee Valley. 'Are you out of your Neanderthal mind?' I yelled at this baboon. 'George could win a race around a baby grand piano!' There is certainly no anti-Moore feeling here in London where George has always been given fantastic publicity. They splashed his fight with Athol Mulley all over the racing pages, and he also had a big play when those negotiations with Murless dragged on and on. And when George got off that plane at London Airport, there was a movie star reception waiting for him. He is big news wherever he goes.

There was one big reason why the British racing public was so excited about the 'Second Coming' of 'Cottonfingers'. After the big Piggott-Murless split, they wanted to see how the Aussie champion stood up to the 'wonderboy' around the terrible Tattenham Corner. Laughing boy Lester did not like seeing Georgie's rump breeze past him on a Murless-trained horse. Lester, naturally, just does not like things like that. When I think of that Derby and George and Lester and the two great colts, I am still staggered by the background drama of it all. There was George riding an equal favourite, a colt Lester was meant to ride, and Piggott sitting up on the other strongest challenger. Man, that was no English Derby, it was another battle of Waterloo.

You may not have learned much about picking winners in this chapter, but I hope you have appreciated the importance of knowing the right people, all the background and the gossip. The winners come later. ...

CHAPTER TWO

Jockeys

Some jockeys are so crooked they cannot even lie in bed straight. Others have the intelligence of a demented pigmy. Neither species ever carries The Butterfly's money. Horse racing is a big enough fundamental gamble without increasing the odds against beating the book by trying to guess whether a 'bent' rider is going all out to win or doing his damnedest to lose. Those jockeys who have not even enough upstairs to deliberately throw a race, let alone win one, still have their occasional triumphs; like Christmas Day it has to come around once a year, but you would soon be disillusioned and derelict if you relied on Santa Claus to fill your stocking every day. There are no such things as miracles in the professional punter's Good Book and Lady Luck is another name for the devil's disciple, that double-crossing, fairy-tale female who lures the regular providers of luncheon vouchers for the bookmakers into backing, for example, all Irish named horses because Paddy Me Darling trotted up for Aunt Maria at 25-1 on St. Patrick's Day thirty-three years ago. It is the same two-timing woman who pushes you up to the betting shop counter, encouraging you to play up your winnings when you are showing a profit and really know that to stay is to be sunk. She kids you that she has fallen for you, when all the time she is the bookmaker's mistress. Remember what I told you about business and birds not mixing.

The lesson to be learned is that the brainless jockeys, the insidious and incompetent, all have winners, but the professional backer can afford to miss them. Racing is full of the world's big men, but it is controlled by the Little People, the seven-stone dwarfs, some of them poisoned, who hold the fate of millions of pounds and people in their scraggy, muck-stained hands every day of the week. The law of libel prevents me from naming the crooks and the cretins. Instead, I shall list with comments the only jockeys who ever ride with my money on their backs. This does not mean that all those who are excluded from this chapter fall into one of the two categories I have mentioned, but if the cap fits . . .

It is my easy-earned money and therefore my prerogative to decide which bonny boys should have the privilege of increasing it for me.

It is elementary arithmetic that if jockeys A, B and C ride more winners every season than the rest of the alphabet, then the odds are more in your favour if you confine yourself to investing exclusively in them, instead of sticking your sucker pin among the gallery of goons.

It is not sufficient for me to give you a list of jockeys to follow. After all, many of them will be riding against each other for much of the time. So it is important for you to know as much about them as possible – their riding styles, tracks on which they excel, type of races in which they produce their best, what they have for breakfast and which day of the month they need the rent money.

Here is my list:

LESTER PIGGOTT: Born with a silver saddle in his mouth; whatever superlative you can think of or invent, it applies to lacerating Lester, a fearless jockey who is addicted to winning and who will spare his

mount nothing within reason in pursuit of the winners'
enclosure. As regards method, Lester is a daring
noncomformist. He revels in being a rebel and breaks
all the rules in the style book, and yet is a champion of
champions. Lester is racing's equivalent of cricket's
swashbuckling Colin Milburn, as opposed to the
classical Peter May. He has no time to be elegant and
orthodox; he is too busy winning races! Being a
bean-pole in a trade for shorties, he has to ride very
short. This is both a handicap and an advantage. It is
a disadvantage because the risk of being thrown on the
way to the start or unseated at the barrier just before
the tape goes up is tremendously enhanced. Several
times when the racecourse commentator has said,
'They're off,' it has been a literal description of
Piggott's posture. He has been left watching the race
from a worm's-eye view, with his whip for a shooting
stick. However, Lester's ugly but unique riding pose
is an asset when he is involved in a tight finish, because
he is able to stretch his hands nearer the horse's ears,
forcing its head down just as they cross the line, so
stealing that extra, vital inch. If you watch Piggott
when it is a dog-fight to the finishing line, you will
observe that he puts his whip away about three strides
from the finish and pushes and pulls with his arms like
a frantic trombone player blowing two instruments at
once. This way he generates more power and thrust
than the more orthodox little chappies who do battle
in the final furlong with the whip flicking in one hand,
while the other shakes the reins as if mixing a cocktail.

Apart from Lester's acknowledged brilliance, there
are two other reasons why I always have sweet dreams
when I know that he is carrying my savings the
following day. Firstly, he is dedicated; secondly, he is
as straight as your bank manager's face when you ask

for a loan. Dedicated! What other jockey in the world would ride the winners of the Queen Elizabeth Stakes and King George V Stakes at Royal Ascot and then fly to Wolverhampton to ride a scrubber in a 'seller' the same evening.

Owners and trainers would rather have Lester on their side than in opposition. Therefore, he is always in demand and since he became a freelance he has become a God, being able to pick or discard his rides without fear or favour, and has the racing nobility eating from his magical hands. Make no mistake, Lester Piggott controls many of the big stables in Britain. He tells trainers when they should and should not run their horses, and they respect his judgment, which is second to none. Therefore, whatever and wherever he rides, Piggott is always on the horse everyone has got to beat. This means that to back against him, you must be extra confident of your selection. Lester is particularly worth following when he travels from one meeting to another on the same day. This applies to all jockeys, but especially so with Piggott, because he does not need the money like some of the others. There is one circumstance when he should always be supported, even if your own judgment tells you that he has chosen to partner a three-legged crab. This is when he nominates to ride for a trainer and owner with whom he has no arrangement and when, in the same race, he could be riding for one of his regular connections, such as his father-in-law, Sam Armstrong, or Johnson Houghton.

An example of this was in 1968 when he had no hesitation in agreeing to partner Irish trainer Vincent O'Brien's Sir Ivor in the 2,000 Guineas and The Derby. He won both classics, beating his father-in-law's Petingo into second place in the 2,000 Guineas. Those shrewd observers who got the message cashed in with Piggott's judgment. On August 20, 1968, he steered Petros to an easy victory in the Rose of York Handicap at York at the crazy odds of 11-2 for Newmarket trainer Van Cutsem. It was most unusual for Piggott to ride for Van Cutsem, particularly as his stable jockey Russ Maddock could have ridden Petros at 8 st. 11 lb., the weight it was set to carry.

When Lester was engaged to ride Tiber for Jeremy Tree, instead of his father-in-law's Dancing Moss, in the Johnnie Walker Ebor Handicap, at York, on August 21, 1968, the significance of this did not escape the smarties. However, on this occasion he just failed to cope with little Ernie Johnson on Lord Allendale's Alignment. He finished second at 9-1, hardly a bad each-way investment!

These are the times when Piggott must always be followed; punch away at him and take the best of his pickings. I am not suggesting that you should acquire blind faith in Piggott, backing him every day and in every race, but make yourself comfortable and wait for the 'strange' rides. If you think he has chosen the wrong horse, give him the benefit of the doubt. I can assure you that he *will* be right, certainly *not you*.

Lester, who had to be better than anyone else to survive because he has a speech impediment and is partly deaf, which prevents him from hearing what is going on behind, has ridden winners in every country he has visited, including Jamaica, America, Australia, France, Germany, Italy and Belgium.

SANDY BARCLAY: A softly spoken Scottish laddie who is endowed with everything necessary to become a champion. All he needs to do for the next twenty years is bank regularly and he will have vast wealth in the

The Butterfly in action at Sandown Park

Above: The Butterfly
when he was on the
other side of the fence –
making a book back
home in Australia.
Right: The Butterfly,
the one without the
disguise, shows off his
cufflinks

stuff that buys bread as well as in talent. Sandy's riding
style is a bit of everything and everyone, he apes no
one, is an intelligent thinker during a race and he will
keep on improving until he has carved a name for
himself among the great men of the turf. Being able to
ride at 7 st. 10 lb. he has a huge advantage over Piggott.

Despite being a fly-weight, he loses nothing in
strength and drive. Barclay is one of the first jockeys
all trainers try to engage when they think that they
have a chance. So for the professional punter, Barclay
is a Fairy Godmother; a real live money-spinner. When
he is on a horse I really fancy, I hear sweet music in
my ears. Barclay should be followed in particular when
a trainer for whom he rarely rides makes a point of
booking him for a big race. What a fantastic judge of
both human and animal flesh is his boss Noel Murless!
His last three jockeys have been Piggott, Australian
champion George Moore and now Barclay. Murless
has the best of all worlds – horses, jockeys, owners and
training facilities. So whatever Barclay is partnering
from his own stable, you can rest assured that it is in the
Rolls Royce class; purring, pretty and powerful. Sandy
is usually very successful at Ascot and Goodwood.

RON HUTCHINSON: A natural light-weight who has
never been lucky in the classics, but who should
always ride a hundred winners every season. Ron,
known affectionately as 'The Happy Horseman', works
very hard and is a grand family man with a lovely wife
and four children. In my opinion, he is Australia's
number one ambassador of the saddle. He is a top
tradesman in the art of riding, but he just lacks that
touch of instinctive genius and is not so electrifying as
Piggott. One point to note is that Hutchinson is very
popular among the public and is extremely poor value

C

on the Tote. Television viewers love him because they can always identify him in a race by his continual bobbing style. He is a cheerful little fellow and attracts a lot of housewives' bets. His style is tidy and immaculate; a joy to watch. The Duke and Duchess of Norfolk have first claim on his services and when he is up on one of their short-priced mounts he should always be backed, especially at Brighton. Goodwood is another course where 'Hutch' is often successful.

JIMMY LINDLEY: This is one British jockey I admire greatly. He has sound judgment and is probably the strongest jockey in a finish riding in England. Yes, that is including Piggott. This poor bonny boy has terrifying weight problems and during recent years he has been plagued with illness. For some inexplicable reason he has never been a favourite of the racing public, but to a professional, like myself, he is a Father Christmas. Because of his unpopularity, he is fantastic value for the Tote punters. Jimmy, who is retained by Jeremy Tree, is restricted because he cannot ride below 8 st. 7 lb., but when one of his stable's horses is fancied quietly in the market, then get on without delay. He is always worth watching at Newmarket.

BILL WILLIAMSON: To Australian turf-goers, he is known as 'Weary Willy'. He is without a doubt the best Australian export riding in Britain. Williamson had an outstanding record in Victoria before coming to Britain in 1960. He is a very cool customer and a fabulous judge of pace, and was renowned 'Down Under' for the art of playing the waiting game. If you cash in on Billy, don't have a heart attack if he is not to be seen as they sweep around the home turn. He knows exactly where to be at every inch of the track and, more important, his eye is never off the winning post. Just as you are about to start offering to collect glasses in one of the racecourse bars to earn your fare home, along breezes 'Weary Willy' to snatch the race by the width of a swollen gland. Your doctor will tell you that he is no good for your blood-pressure, but your bank manager will love him. Like Lindley, he is not popular with the racing public and is wonderful value on the Tote.

He has a neat copybook style and is equally out-standing on all tracks and over any distance. If you think the horse is good enough and Williamson is riding, you have more than enough security to ask for a loan. York is a course for which he has a special liking.

RUSS MADDOCK: Born in Queensland, Australia, Russ is another natural light-weight. Like Hutchinson, he is industrious, more than competent, and a genuine professional. One of his trademarks is his ability to use the whip equally effectively with either hand. He is particularly outstanding on sharp tracks, such as Chester, Alexandra Park and Kempton Park. Russ rode with success in Singapore before coming to Britain to ride for Pat Rohan in the north. Russ, a good all-rounder, then became based in Newmarket with Bernard Van Cutsem. He is continually riding track work and is fantastically keen, never venturing far from the horses in his stable and taking a personal interest in all the charges in his governor's yard. Do not forget that Russ is worth a couple of lengths start on those sharp tracks which I have named above.

YVRES ST. MARTIN: The 'jockey of the Gods' as the French call him. Although riding most of the time in France, he is worth mentioning because on occasions he appears on British circuits and when he does it is like popping a magnum of champagne; he fairly sparkles and effervesces, a luxury to the palate for the racing connoisseur. A handsome young man with a dashing style to match his good looks, this is Mr Supremo of all the premier jockeys in the world. Yvres is supremely confident, rides very short and very seldom goes for the whip, but when he does he is extremely accomplished. He has won international races all over the world and will be remembered for his stimulating victory on Relko in the English Derby. Whenever he partners anything in Britain for his boss Frances Mathet, he has a start over the rest as long as de Gaulle's nose. I am sure you will agree with me, he must be some jockey!

JOE MERCER: A really top flight English jockey whom I would always prefer to be riding with my money rather than against it. A very personable fellow, he gives nothing away in a race and is punishing with the stick. He rides plenty of staying horses for the Astor family and is a long distance specialist. Joe has a remarkable record at Bath, Salisbury, and Chepstow, and can always be relied upon to be paying frequent visits to the winners' enclosure at these meetings. Mercer is another of those jockeys like Williamson and Lindley who should be backed on the Tote, except at Bath, Salisbury and Chepstow, where he is so popular.

GEOFF LEWIS: Known in racing as the 'Welsh Wizard', he is forceful and strong and typifies as well as anyone the driving, tough English style of race-riding. Unlike many of his contemporaries, he has no real claim to fame in major events and he failed to score even once out of two working visits to Australia. However, he is retained by two strong stables, those of

John Sutcliffe, Jnr, and Staff Ingham, and often rides for
the Queen. One of his happy hunting grounds is Cal-
cutta, where he often goes during the English winter.
More to the point, when he is on a well-backed horse,
especially a two-year-old trained by Ingham, it is as hot
as any Madras curry he might have during his trips to
India. Geoff has proved himself the master of the switch-
back courses, such as Epsom, Brighton and Lingfield.

FRANKIE DURR: Another natural light-weight who
in 1968 enjoyed his best season ever. For many years
he has been a good average performer who has proved
himself competent over all distances and all courses.
Distinctive because of his American crouched tech-
nique, he has matured into a reliable tradesman who
can be trusted to bring home the bread. He has been
in more demand since he became connected with David
Robinson's horses which are trained privately at
Newmarket by Michael Jarvis and Paul Davey. You
will normally find him engaged to ride a much-fancied
contender for a big handicap.

GREVILLE STARKEY: Here we have a really top class
English jockey. He knows exactly where he is in a race
and is a brilliant judge. Although perhaps not quite so
powerful as Lindley, nevertheless, he is very difficult
to beat in a hard fought finish. The racing public must
consist of many strange animals, because Greville is
far from popular, which makes him a rosy proposition
on the Tote. I can best sum up Starkey by saying that
if he is riding a mount I fancy, then I put on a little
more than I would normally.

ERIC ELDIN: One of the most vigorous jockeys in
Britain. He rides very short, has a peculiar action when
going for the whip, but is a flying machine in a gruelling

battle for the line. My advice to all punters is become one of his disciples and follow him almost with blind faith when he goes to spread the work at provincial tracks.

PETER ROBINSON: An opportunist who often dashes his mount to the front half a mile from home and leaves the rest of the field tottering behind like a dozy lot of bridesmaids who have lost sight of the bride. Peter stars on northern circuits like Ripon, Ayr and Beverley, but he does not get the opportunities he deserves.

DUNCAN KEITH: A cheerful, bright boy, I expect Duncan to go on to bigger things now that he has established himself with the Peter Walwyn stable. In 1968 he had a very successful season after suffering some bad injuries in recent years. He appears to go well on all tracks and is on the upgrade.

BRIAN TAYLOR: Similar in many characteristics to Piggott, Taylor is a forceful and versatile rider who seems to excel particularly over a long journey. Based at Newmarket with the Harvey Leader stable, he is a prolific producer of winners at Yarmouth and Newmarket.

STAN CLAYTON: The Queen's jockey who is retained by Newmarket trainer Bruce Hobbs. Stan, a Yorkshireman, is efficient on all courses, but he seems to produce his best in races over one and a half miles and above. And when he does show them the way home, it is usually at a very sweet price.

TAFFY THOMAS: Probably one of the best English light-weights, he is equally at home on sprinters and stayers. Thomas is Geoffrey Barling's stable jockey at

Newmarket and he has the asset of being small but strong. Providing his waistline does not expand with his bank balance, Taffy should have a bright future as one of Britain's most sought after light-weights.

EDDIE HIDE: For many years champion of the north, Eddie now has succeeded 'Scobie' Breasley as first jockey to Sir Gordon Richards. By northern standards, he is in the highest echelons and I see no reason why he should not attain the same status in the south where it is more demanding and exacting.

JOHNNY SEAGRAVE: Now that Hide has moved south, Seagrave looks like taking over as Cock of the North for many years to come. He is lucky enough to be riding regularly for Pat Rohan, who turns out winners as consistently as Monday follows Sunday. Johnny has a pleasant habit of landing hat-tricks at night meetings and it is worth investing in doubles and trebles on him when he has a number of fancied rides. Courses where he always shines are Ripon, Beverley and Catterick.

DAVID MAITLAND: A competent boy who copied, to a large extent, the Australian crouch of Hutchinson when he was understudy to 'Hutch'. He is quite capable, although so far he has not quite crossed the bridge from apprentice to fully fledged jockey.

Of the apprentices, four deserve a mention. They are Ernie Johnson, Tony Murray, Richard Dicey and Raymond Still. Johnson is a mature judge, a good thinker and a strong finisher. Dicey is brilliant at the barrier, while Still is a natural light-weight who has improved tremendously. But the one, in my opinion, with the greatest future is Murray, who is more of an all-round horseman.

CHAPTER THREE

Trainers

Trainers have to be a combination of nanny, tutor and diplomat. The horses in their care have to be cleaned, fed and taught how to behave like gentlemen or ladies on the racecourse. The need for being something of a diplomat is useful when the trainer has to explain to an irate owner why the goat masquerading in a racehorse's carcass, for which he paid all of £65, failed to win the Derby.

Some trainers could not even house-train a poodle, let alone break-in a horse and prepare it for racing. Others have such a twisted outlook, they cannot see the end of their nose, except when finding the way to the bank. A crooked trainer engaging a crooked jockey to ride a dishonest horse is not The Butterfly's idea of a safe wager. The trainer probably suspects the jockey of skulduggery, the jockey has the same fears about the trainer and they both end up being double-crossed by the horse which has different plans from both of them.

I rely on a few leading trainers to provide my eggs and bacon. But one of the jockeys I have described in the previous chapter must always be riding and all the other conditions, such as the type of meeting, the sort of race and the weather, must be right.

Here is my list of trainers to follow:

VINCENT O'BRIEN: If ever God gave a gift to racing, it was Ireland's Vince O'Brien. This unassuming and

sincere little Irishman creates champions with the
artistic touch of a Michelangelo. If racing is the sport
of kings, then O'Brien wears the largest crown. It is
hardly necessary for me to say that, in my opinion,
this superman is the greatest trainer in the world.
Admittedly, he buys only the best meat, but from it he
produces the most appetising dishes ever to appear on
racecourses. To look down a list of his horses and all
the breeding data is like browsing through an animal's
edition of *Who's Who*. His headquarters at Ballyboyle
House, in County Cashel, is more of a recluse than a
racing establishment. In this quiet, emerald paradise,
he goes unobtrusively and diligently about his business
of preparing for raids on the classics, which are his
main objective every season. Although he has won
every classic race, he does not command the public
following of someone like Paddy Prendergast, but the
people closest to racing show him the respect reserved
for men who somehow seem to be a little more than
human. He always hires the top jockeys – numerous
Australians have ridden for him in the past – and so it
is the best being put with the best and producing the
best. Whenever a horse trained by O'Brien goes out,
even if it has never seen a racecourse before and no
matter what the odds, you can rest assured that it will
very nearly collect the biscuits.

NOEL MURLESS: His record boasts enough without
anyone else having to do it for him. Every year his
stock are the blue-blood of racehorses. They are royal
in breeding, regal in appearance, princely in performance and collect prize money as if it were taxes. Most
of the charges in his care are privately bred, so he is
assured of having champions in his large Newmarket
yard every season. Most of his horses are classic

material, so he goes for handicaps only very rarely. He produces his two-year-olds late, but when they do run they are not just taking a peek at the scenery. You can be sure that they are perfectly tuned up and are cherry ripe to win. Any starter from the Murless stable is recognised as a good proposition for the professional punter. Each Murless runner is like a new brand of baked beans; it will have undergone every conceivable test at home before being placed on the market. The Murless stable is a supermarket of champions, but when you invest in his stock you get more than green shield stamps in return. Like Vincent O'Brien, he has time only for the best jockeys. Piggott rode for him for a number of years until the so-called happiest of marriages in racing floundered on the rocks with Lester turning freelance. Australia's George Moore was the next to hold the coveted post and he was followed by the superlative youngster, Sandy Barclay. A combination of Murless, Barclay and a horse whose famous dad slept with an equally famous mum is very hard to beat, especially at Epsom and Ascot. An example of the value of the Murless horses is Connaught. Although finishing second to Sir Ivor in the 1968 English Derby, it had won only one small race in its life by the mid-summer of that year, yet £200,000 would not have been enough to buy it.

PADDY PRENDERGAST: This man must be given the respect of Napoleon whenever he brings an invasion party over from his Irish training establishment. But they must be backed only when they are a short market order, say 6–4 or 5–2 in the betting. There is always a ring of confidence when Paddy has a really 'good 'un'. The Little People on the course start fetching out £100 notes, bore everyone around them with a lot of old blarney and generally act as if they are just about to win their first ever war or something. Since the beginning of the 1960s, Prendergast's record in near classical meetings has been outstanding, although he did not enjoy so much success in 1967 and 1968. However, the fame of Meadow Court and Ragusa will last for ever, but if you are depending on racing for a living it is no use dwelling in the past. Yesterday's winners are history. What is going to win today or tomorrow is the only concern of the professional bettor. So it is much better to be a clairvoyant than a historian. Paddy is always a big buyer at the yearling sales in America, Dublin and Newmarket, and everything he purchases is of supreme quality. Most of the eighty-odd horses which he has in his stable every season are two- or three-year-olds, which means he is certain to have at least a couple of potential classic winners every year. His two-year-olds are always perfectly mannered. They do their jobs beautifully and never mess about like some of the other ill-mannered frogs we see on our racecourses. In fact, all of his animals look a picture in the paddock.

STAFF INGHAM: Here we have a really astute judge, a former successful National Hunt rider who has transformed into a really first-class trainer on the flat. The connections of the Ingham stable at Epsom are noted for their big gambles and very few mistakes are made at this quarter. This type of stable is ideal for the racing public, because you do not have to be able to tell which is the jockey and which is the horse to back *all* the winners Ingham sends out. When 'friends' of this stable put their money down, the horse wins. He should especially be followed in two-year-old races . . . when the price is right. And by 'right' I mean very short. If the cash suddenly floods for an Ingham horse in that sort of race, it will usually oblige. Remember, a 5-4 winner is far healthier than a 100-1 loser. Staff never aims at the classics. In fact, he does not ever have that type of horse in his yard, but concentrates on the better class handicaps. Whenever possible, he engages Lewis to ride for him on the flat, but occasionally he uses Hutchinson. Sometimes he runs a horse over the jumps and when he does he will always pick up a prize with it, Geordie Ramshaw or Jim Uttley usually getting it home for him.

GEORGE TODD: A trainer of the old brigade, George is a specialist with aged geldings in minor handicaps or selling races. The thing to look for with this stable is a 'springer' gamble; a horse being backed down from 8-1 to 3-1. When this happens it is always caused by inspired money because this is another stable which has a number of very heavy betting owners. Never be put off if an apprentice is riding. George nearly always relies on one of his own boys to do the job, who can claim a five or seven pound allowance. I can promise you the lad will be as well schooled as the horse, and that is saying something. An example of how George keeps old geldings in training and earning their keep is Caught Out, who won when he was sixteen years old and looked as fit as a three-year old. He very rarely has a two-year-old in his yard and more than half of his stock are geldings which are getting a bit old in the hoof. However, he did win the St.Leger and Irish Derby with Sodium, but from the punter's angle his runners in minor handicaps will be most rewarding.

CAPTAIN RYAN PRICE: A fantastic horse master who has always a giant stock in training, Ryan has built up

a world-wide reputation with his jumpers. In the past
he has never bothered with the flat, but in 1968 he
proved himself equally proficient at the summer game.
The Price stable at Findon in Sussex is renowned for its
'old fashioned' gambles and any hard market move for
one of his charges is a definite signal for you to reap
the golden harvest waiting to be picked. He may have
reached only the rank of captain in the service, but he
is a Field-Marshal when it comes to leading a coup on
the racecourse. Many of the stable's owners are big
backers and 'The Captain' is an expert at preparing his
horses for major races. Races like the Schweppes
Trophy, and big hurdle races at Newbury and Cheltenham are his speciality, especially when there is an
ante-post betting market. Over the sticks his horses
should only be supported when champion Josh Gifford
is riding. If the price of one of his charges drops
dramatically overnight in any ante-post market, then
get on without waiting to consult your horoscope.
Never mind whether you are a Cancer or a clown,
Ryan Price is the star to follow when the connections
of his stable have brought out all their hoarded pieces
of eight. As with Paddy Prendergast's horses, never
back them unless they are fancied in the betting.

At meetings like Plumpton, Fontwell, Wye, Newton
Abbot and Wincanton invariably he wins with short-
priced favourites. On the flat he has given most rides
to the promising boy, Tony Murray, another gamble
which has paid off.

MAJOR DICK HERN: One of the new breed of trainers,
Dick has the ability to produce two-year-olds fully
trained and raring to go and win the first time out.
This is an old art and a very rare gift these days. There
are always about seventy horses in his yard at West

Ilsey, Berkshire, and the majority of them are bred to stay extreme distances. Hern is my idea of a really complete trainer. He built up quite a reputation for himself while training for the Holliday family and he has consolidated his position among the highest echelons since his association with the Astors. He has been unlucky in so much that his horses have been struck down repeatedly by viruses, such as the cough, but if ever he completes a season without any training setbacks, I am convinced that he will be one of Britain's leading trainers. Never be dissuaded from backing a horse from Hern's stable just because it has never run. I can promise you that every time a horse goes on a racecourse from Dick's yard, it is running for its supper. Obviously I am not suggesting you should back every runner from this stable. But if you make an animal from this yard the form horse at the weights and under the conditions (i.e. the going and the track), then support it with the confidence of a poker player using marked cards. Knowing when to back his two-year-olds first time out is more complicated, but generally they are worth following if entered in a race in which on their breeding they should outclass their rivals. He trains horses for the Queen, which says something for his standing in the racing world.

SAM ARMSTRONG: This Newmarket trainer always has a big heap of horses in his yard and he usually wins more races each season than anyone else in Britain. His stock are always well turned out and he is prepared to send them any distance to lift a prize. Sometimes they start at such ridiculous odds as 10-1 on, which is a joke from the betting angle, but they still collect the fodder money. Most of his achievements come with three-year-olds, but always he has a few older horses which are sent out penny-pinching in middle-class handicaps up and down the country. Sam probably has the largest set of international owners in racing and the stable is noted for its betting connections. When Sam engages his son-in-law, Lester Piggott, to ride for him and the money goes down as if the owners of the notes are getting new tenners for old fivers, there are two things that you should do. Firstly, ring up your bookmaker and tell him not to forget to go to the bank. Secondly, book yourself a fortnight's holiday in Spain and if the travel agent demands a deposit just leave him your betting slip – it will be the safest security you will ever possess.

HARRY WRAGG: Another Newmarket trainer who has owners from all over the world. Harry, a former brilliant jockey, gears his training programme so that his horses reach their peak for Royal Ascot, New-market and York meetings. His stock should be ignored early in the season, especially two-year-olds which develop late. But when a couple of his horses have trotted in and it is obvious that most of his charges must be just about 'right', then cash in where only fools would fear to tread. Harry, who is the only trainer I know in Britain to time horses on the gallops, is unique in the skill of prolonging a horse's racing life. He manages to keep bringing in prize money with oldish horses in fairly top grade handicaps. Wragg's stable is not noted for big gambles, so many of his winners are returned at attractive odds. So if you fancy a Wragg-trained horse, back it whatever the price in the betting market. Harry buys from all around the world and mainly employs Australian jockeys, although usually on short-term engagements.

RYAN JARVIS: This Newmarket stable is often full of mediocre-type horses, but Ryan is one of the most able trainers at placing his animals to win races. He will travel, like Armstrong, all over the land if he thinks that he can pick up a pot. Honestly, I think he would rocket a horse to the moon if he believed that there was racing life there. This is a stable to follow on the betting board. There are a number of fair bettors with horses in the yard and, if there is a market move for a Ryan Jarvis-trained horse, crash in and keep punching away until the bookies cannot take any more punishment. Ryan is particularly clever at placing three-year-olds in minor handicaps. If he does not think that he can win a race at Carlisle, say, he will take it to a night meeting at Warwick, or trek all the way from Newmarket up to Ayr or down to Salisbury. When he does make an all-day excursion, the message is as good as if he wrote you a personal 'wish you were here' card. He often uses an apprentice, but relies mainly on Eric Eldin, although there is no official retainer in existence between them.

BERNARD VAN CUTSEM: Lord Derby's trainer heads a stable which has owners who bet with the crown jewels. When this yard has a 'certainty', it is like a run on Wall Street. Money descends as if some lunatic has just felled, in one sweep, all those trees on which it grows. So the lesson for the punter to learn, where this Newmarket stable is concerned, is follow the lolly. Van Cutsem owns a number of the horses in his yard. He is a good all-rounder and gives two-year-olds plenty of time. When he sends something up north, it has a great chance. After all, no one goes to the Pole just to catch a cold. This man makes very few errors. Willy Carson rides all of Lord Derby's horses and Russ

Left: A fancy dress ball on board the *Queen Mary* during a cruise to celebrate The Butterfly's fortune won on Sea Bird in the English Derby. *Below:* The Butterfly leaving one of his favourite night spots, the bill having been paid by the bookies

The Butterfly proving he is no backseat driver

Maddock partners the rest. Both are capable of doing the job.

SIR GORDON RICHARDS: Knighted for being Mr Wonderful of jockeys, Sir Gordon has made a valuable contribution to the training ranks. He does not normally give board and lodgings to real champions, but he wins his fair share of good races. He should be followed at Salisbury, Bath and Newbury. He very seldom takes a horse to Newmarket or up north, but if he does it is a really good thing; something worth securing a second mortgage on. Contrary to popular belief, this is not a betting stable. Now that 'Scobie' Breasley has retired, all the pick of the rides will go to Eddie Hide, who has left the Elsey yard in Yorkshire for this plum posting.

IAN BALDING: An amateur rider himself, Ian has some beautifully bred horses in his care, some of them owned by the Queen. His favourite courses are Newbury, Salisbury, Bath and Ascot. This is not a gambling stable and some of his winners 'go in' at a nice price. Paul Cook is now the stable jockey.

JOHN DUNLOP: Training for the Duke and Duchess of Norfolk at Arundel is one of the most envied jobs in racehorse training. Since taking over from Gordon Smyth, Dunlop has met with moderate success. The horses are mostly home-bred and the stable is very 'hot' with two-year-olds. Mostly they are kept for Brighton, where the Duke is a steward of the meeting, Goodwood, Lingfield and Newbury. When this stable has a really good proposition, there is the same ring of confidence on the course as with Paddy Prendergast horses. On these occasions, one should charge in and

D

begin to live like a Duke. Dunlop does train for a few outside owners and they are all ridden by the stable's jockey, Ron Hutchinson.

DOUG SMITH: Although a newcomer to training, Doug deserves a mention because of an incredible first season in 1968. He has taken over most of Geoffrey Brook's connections at Newmarket for whom he used to ride during his celebrated career as a jockey. It is obvious that he is running the horses scrupulously honestly. Therefore, when the Form Book points to one of his stock being 'well in', then there is no need to worry whether or not it will be trying. All of his horses are triers, which is saying something these days. He is not afraid to put up a boy and, occasionally, he goes in with a bonanza-priced winner. I see no reason why he should not go on to bigger and better things.

CHAPTER FOUR

On-Course Betting

Anyone who is interested in making racing pay must remember that the racecourse is his office and not his club. Socialising on the track is strictly for the amateurs. A surgeon does not get himself cockeyed during a delicate operation and neither should the professional punter while operating on the racecourse. There are two breeds of people who go racing. There are those who go to give money away and those who go to collect it. By now there is no need to tell you to which group The Butterfly belongs. If Lady Horseface wants to get stinking, that is her business. Probably she has her seventeenth husband as well insured as the previous sixteen and need not be too worried about the future, even if she does back all six losers. Most women go racing to show off their latest exotic creations, while the men just show off. Without the men, the women would feel undressed. And the bookmakers go along because they know that for every one Butterfly there will be a thousand clowns like I have just mentioned.

Have you ever heard of anyone receiving an income tax demand for £100 and immediately cracking a bottle of champagne? No, well at the racecourse you will witness the equivalent every afternoon. Nut upon nut will place a £100 credit bet with their bookmaker, watch their crocodile crawl in last and go straight to the bar and order a bottle of bubbly for each of his friends. Then in comes that Lady Horseface and says, 'Darling, did you back Go Slow? By jove, didn't it just live up to its name! You simply must have a drink on me.' If the same people saw reason to celebrate the same sort of transaction in their business, they would be strapped in a straitjacket long before they had a chance to go bankrupt. Do not worry, The Butterfly has his carnival days, but never during business hours. And business hours for me are between the first and last races each day.

Every racecourse is like a little Soho where pimps and peers brush shoulders and indulge together in the same vice. Bookmakers are very democratic people. They will take money from anyone. It does not matter which drawer your mother came out of, just providing that the cash comes from the right mint.

The most important point the professional backer must remember is that when he passes through the gates into the racing enclosure he is clocking on. Once on the inside, then the only consideration must be business. The bars must be avoided as if they are filled with carbon dioxide . . . and most of the talk in them is more deadly than any poisonous gas. All over the place you hear such Christian and charitable comments as, 'Did you see that dirty, little, fiddling . . . ?' or 'Those bent little b . . . should be crucified.'

The truth is that there is far less villainy in British racing than the public supposes. Jockeys, as the racing public knows, can, and do, make mistakes, but this does not mean that they are deliberately throwing a race. Many shop assistants, bus conductors and taxi drivers short-change customers, but only a handful of them do it intentionally.

Any hard-up solicitor's clerk could make a fortune by setting up business in a racecourse bar and serving

writs, instead of nips, on behalf of slandered jockeys.
While the mugs compete feverishly in the Silly Stories
Stakes in the bars, The Butterfly and anybody else
who was not born yesterday – believe me you would
be amazed at the number of births yesterday! – are
down at the paddock watching the horses parade. This
is most important and every animal should be inspected
closely before each race. There are special points that
you should be looking for and it is imperative to
scrutinise each horse as if it is under a microscope. For
a start, any horse that you are considering backing
should, first and foremost, be a good walker. Yes,
deportment is just as necessary for a racehorse as for a
Christian Dior fashion model. A good walker is a
horse whose hind legs almost overlap its front legs
while parading. If a horse is going to do its best it
must be feeling well. When a human being is in good
health it is usually reflected in the face, by the com-
plexion and the skin. A horse reveals how it is feeling
in its coat. If it is raring to go, its coat will be smooth,
glistening and running the right way. The head will
be held high and erect, and the eyes will be clear and
alert. As soon as any horse starts to 'break out' – the
official term for sweating up – cross it off your list
immediately. If you back it, you will be the one
sweating long before the end of the race. Other danger
signs to watch for are horses wearing boots, bandages
or elastic plasters. It is hard enough finding the horses
in perfect condition which are going to win without
laying out sympathy money on 'things' that need the
help of armoured protection and artificial limbs. The
only exception to this rule is when a horse wears
blinkers for the first time. I always put money on a
horse in these circumstances because its performance
always improves when wearing blinkers on the first

occasion. However, most genuine champions do not need the assistance of wings or helmets . . . or even jockeys.

As soon as the horses leave the paddock, you must hurry to the rails to observe them cantering down to the start. Be on the look-out for an attractive mover, which means a long, gliding stride. Forget about any animal which seems to think it is playtime, or is acting as if giving some little chap a free lift is an indignity. Usually the jockey ends up with the more hurt pride . . . not to mention *his* backside or *your* pocket.

Watch for a horse knuckling down to its work and full of running. There are many dogs in this world without going out of your way to be bitten by one. . . .

Now come the most vital minutes of all, when the betting reaches a climax. Get yourself positioned in the territory I have named as No-Man's Land. It's that barren stretch of concrete that separates the bookies who bet on the members' rail and those who use the conventional blackboards and satchels. At the top end of this space you will see a cluster of racecourse representatives – the men who receive code messages, via the tic tac men, from their bookmaker bosses in credit offices and betting shops. When a message comes in, The Butterfly is there. I do not try to decipher the code. I simply follow the representative, who may have £1,000 to invest. Sooner or later the representative must speak to a bookie. You follow the representative; there is no law against it.

The message may order him to place £500 on a 10-1 shot, or £5,000 on a short favourite. This money is always 'hot'. Sooner or later the representative has to start putting it on. Now he has to speak in plain English. As soon as you know the horse, you, too, can join the gold rush before the odds are drastically shortened.

Observe the betting movements as if it is a draft in a sales office. This is where all the answers are to be found. A market move for a horse, which has satisfied you in the paddock and on the way to the barrier, is confirmation that the people who count in racing also share your view. Follow the combination of a good jockey and an in-form horse, particularly those that do well at certain tracks. 'Horses for courses' is an old racing saying. Like the old Chinaman, it is also very wise. Never back a horse that is drawn badly. Horses do win occasionally from poor positions, but when they do you and The Butterfly can afford to miss the treat.

When you have made your irrevocable decision, get yourself up in the Gods of the grandstand where many prayers are recited, but few are answered. Down below there will be a flock of frantic men shouting, signalling and gesticulating in a baffling scene of feverish activity. It could be an auction which has become out of control, or a get-together of a dozen different protest groups. Suddenly the public announcement echoes crisp and clear, 'They're under Starter's orders.'

The commotion and confusion will cease quite suddenly, like a raging sea turning instantly into a patient pool as the storm abates. The stadium becomes shrouded in silence. This is the moment of great expectations. Just the sound of heavy, communal breathing, like a thousand bellows expanding and contracting in harmony. A thousand sets of narrowed eyes squinting through binoculars, all trained in one direction, the spot on the far side where the animals are assembled at the barrier. All the faces are taut and tense. In less than two minutes some will be lit up, while the majority will be all sick looking. This is instant life; few win, while the rest lose. The only difference is that on a racecourse the winners and the losers are rejected in seconds, whereas in life one has to wait a lifetime for the result.

'They're off!' The tapes rise and the horses begin their stampede, with the jockeys poised over their backs like unrelenting slave masters. The horses swing into the home straight.

'Now with less than three furlongs to go it is Indian Major from Saucy Sandy and Big Bad Billy . . . ' the commentator goes on in an unemotional monotone, which seems so incongruous amid the tingling, razor-edge atmosphere. As the horses sprint into the final furlong in front of the grandstand with every muscle taut and whips cracking down on hard, glistening hides in a desperate charge for the winning post, every inhibition goes with the wind amid the air of gripping excitement. The hush is shattered by a mighty roar, like the climax to a symphony concert which has been heard in respectful quiet until the signal for the final ovation.

'Go on Sandy!' . . . 'Good old Lester!' . . . 'Go on my little darling!' . . . No one honestly believes that their cries and pleadings have any effect, or will be heard on the track, but it is an outlet for the tension which has been trapped and forcibly held down inside them.

'Photograph,' says the same cold, detached voice of the commentator. Then the excited speculation begins; which one of the horses in the photograph finish has won? Five minutes later, the announcer's voice cuts short every conversation.

'Here is the result of the last race. First, number

three; second, number nine; and third, number one. The distances were a short head and a neck.'

Most people screw up their tickets and grind them into the turf. Then comes a further announcement. 'There is a stewards' inquiry into the last race. The public are advised to retain their betting tickets in case the result is reversed.'

People immediately start searching the ground for discarded slips of paper like fanatics in an anti-litter campaign. They would need to disqualify the first half dozen before most of them would have a chance of winning. The professional never throws away a betting slip until after the 'weigh-in', even if his horse is last of eighty-six runners. You never know!

The importance of knowing all the different riding styles, which I have dealt with in the chapter on jockeys, is for making it easier to read a race. I do not bother about checking colours. Instead, I pick out the runners according to the various riding styles. My eyesight earns me my living. At the end of a race you will never see The Butterfly's glasses trained on the one in front. I am always watching that battle for third, fourth or fifth berth. Forget the first two. You can read all about them in the newspapers the following morning.

To be a successful professional you must be conservative. To get out of one's depth is to drown. That is the first lesson when learning to swim – the first and last when learning to bet. You must be modest at the outset. This is a good game provided you play it slow, play it steady, play it cool. You have got to be with it or very soon you will be without it.

Sometimes, if I see a short-priced favourite with a bad 'jock', I'll lay it to the bookies at over the odds, which is the same as backing the remainder of the field at a collective price. If you are to survive in this jungle, full of greedy savages, you must be calm and cautious. I munch through three or four packets of chewing gum every day.

There should be no limit to the amount you can win, but you *must* apply a strict limit on your daily losses. Ignore newspaper tips. Certainly you may read the racing journalists' articles for the latest tittle-tattle, but never back another man's opinion. Never become a compulsive, every day punter. Confine yourself to meetings you have studied, or a race that you fancy. The bookies love the man who punts away all his winnings.

A late riding change announced on the course can be very significant if a top jockey 'goes up' at the eleventh hour to replace a boy. Remember, remember, it is better to study the form fully for one race than to bet on insufficient information through the card. The most efficient and uncomplicated way to assess a race is to begin by deleting the horses which, in your view, just cannot win. Sometimes a rabbit will hop in, but to try to predict such outsiders winning is like attempting to forecast the British weather. If in doubt, and you must bet, support the 'springer' – the horse that shortens dramatically in the betting just before the off.

Never count your winnings until you are home in bed. During the National Hunt season take your afternoon siesta during those all-amateur slap-stick comedy acts, in which most riders are ex-cavalry officers. Solomon could not pick the winner among that lot.

Late money for horses trained by Ingham, Todd, Van Cutsem, Rohan, F. Cundell and Sutcliffe, Jnr, is always good enough to win me over to their side. W.

Marshall is a specialist in 'sellers', both on the flat and over the sticks. When his platers are 'ready', they are always supported with fanatical enthusiasm. For example, in the 1967–68 National Hunt season, Malacca, one of his novice hurdlers, was backed down from 33–1 to 5–1. This particular horse tumbled through all fractions in the betting like a never-ending avalanche. Stable jockey Ron Atkins did the 'job', driving Malacca past the post first in a desperate finish which must have had many hearts fluttering. The gamble came off, as do most of those originating from connections of the Marshall yard. During the same season, they entered a horse called New Conqueror in a selling hurdle race at Doncaster. Now on the flat this well-bred animal out of Tamerlane had won over seven furlongs at Lingfield as a two-year-old, and in its later years had carried an enormous amount of weight to victory in a handicap at Ally Pally, the nickname for London's Alexandra Park track, while trained by John Bartholmew, at Southfleet, in Kent. If New Conqueror had known that he was competing in a 'seller', I am sure the poor fellow would have died of shame. Needless to say, it won at a short price. You don't need to be as cute as The Butterfly to back winners like that in a 'seller'. Certainly the returned price was cramped, but you would have more than doubled your investment. I have yet to come across the bank which would give you better interest than that for your money. New Conqueror went on to win a good handicap for Mr Marshall. A horse like New Conqueror, which is dropped in class, usually constitutes a sound wager.

The art of betting is being able to achieve value for money. It is all a matter of buying and selling at the right price. A jeweller knows the value of a ring and, no matter how much you plead, he will not go above that price to buy it from you, unless he wants to go the same way as mug punters. If Lester Piggott rides three winners, his fourth mount will be, say, 2-1 when its legitimate odds are 10-1. The false price is caused by all the doubles, trebles and yankees which have accumulated from betting shops all over Britain. This is a common example of shocking value. The price in this case has nothing whatsoever to do with the true chances of the horse. So The Butterfly, in that kind of situation, opposes the false favourite and tries to 'lay' it at 5-2, a half-point more than the bookies are offering. This is called trading. It really means that I turn bookmaker for a race. Betting that a horse will lose is still a rare exercise among British punters.

The principle of all horserace betting, whether on the course, in the betting shop, or on the telephone back home, is to beat the market. You must endeavour to anticipate stable moves before they happen. This way you get 7-2 about a horse that eventually starts at 3-1 or 5-2. This makes an enormous amount of difference when gambling in thousands of pounds every year. In fact, it makes the difference between being a Butterfly or a bum. It is all a game of mind-reading, and always being one jump ahead of the others; like most of the hurdlers I back!

CHAPTER FIVE

A Day in the Life of a Professional Punter

My alarm clock is set for 7.30 every morning. It does not matter how late I was returning home the night before, I never lie in bed a minute after the bell sounds for the first round in the new day's fight with the eternal foe. The Butterfly always springs out of his bedroom corner fighting fit, even if he did arrive home with the milkman. I fling open the windows, breathe deeply and look out across London. Men with a rolled brolly in one hand, a newspaper in the other, a slice of unfinished toast dangling from the mouth and, surprisingly, nothing sticking from an ear, are rushing to pack the early morning Tube trains and buses. Thankfully, I am not a part of the crazy, dizzy world in a flat spin beneath my window. There is no Mr Jones waiting with a stop-watch in some artificially-lit office in an artificial world on the 189th floor to check whether I am a hundredth of a second late for work. My first-floor balcony is a gallery. I am a spectator and I have no wish to be a participator in the Mad-Hatter Stakes down below. I am answerable only to myself, and that is worth more than the Bank of England before devaluation and those bits of shiny pieces Her Majesty keeps stashed away in her riverside pad where the guards wear skirts and eat beef. If you think that I am running from ordinary life, you are not strictly right. I am fleeing!

I always feel good at the dawn of a new betting day. It is essential to feel confident and inspired, knowing within yourself that it is going to be another profitable day. Immediately I am fully awake, I make myself a large cup of milk coffee and dive straight into the newspapers. I have no time for politics or the news of any wars. My political knowledge is confined, for example, to knowing that English women were helped in their fight for the vote by somebody who jumped in the path of a Derby favourite at Epsom. If The Butterfly had been on that favourite nothing would have convinced him that the sinning suffragette was not a member of some big bookmaker's suicide squad. If a Prime Minister is assassinated I shall read about it *only* if it happens on a racecourse . . . or if there were an ante-post market on the possibility of it occurring. Sometimes I do squint at the society gossip columns round about the strawberry and cream time of Royal Ascot, just to see if The Butterfly, or one of his well-formed companions, have made a paragraph or two among such world-shattering revelations as Lady Alwaysproducing giving birth to her tenth 'surprise' packet and declaring, 'I just don't know what my husband will say when he returns this week from a ten-year tour of the Far East.'

I study every racing article in all newspapers so that I am familiar with the different views, but I am never wholly influenced by anything I read. If I read that a horse did an impressive gallop the day before, then I know the animal in question is in good condition, but this does not mean it will win. However, half the battle is knowing for sure which horses are ready to run for their lives. There is nothing worse than being on dead meat, a non-trier. So if you see reported that a horse which you fancy has been pleasing its connections at home, then you can bet with confidence, aware that it has been specially tuned-up for the race. If the horse gets beaten, you know that you supported it for the right reasons. In other words, you did your homework thoroughly and abided by the rules. The professional is the skilled labourer as opposed to the unskilled. I know that bad luck does not buy caviare, or even cod, but if you stick to my charter you will win more often than you lose. Providing you conform with this code of conduct in gambling, you can stand the freak results and the bad runs. The secret is being consistent, diligent and as unemotional as a man in a coma. Bookmakers depend on losers chasing their losses and inevitably squandering more and more money, making recovery and survival impossible. The bookmakers cannot contain the punter who punches away systematically, not being influenced by the success or failure of the previous day. This rare breed of punter reverses the law of averages into his favour instead of the bookies'. Making betting a set operation with inflexible laws which must *never* be stretched, let alone broken, is the basis for backing to win regularly.

After memorising everything I have read in the racing pages, including the split infinitives, I start to make telephone calls to all my contacts based at the main training centres throughout Britain. I have something in the region of fifty expert judges on my pay-roll who spend most of their day looking at an inflated world through magnified lenses, just for the financial benefit of yours truly. These astute veterans of the turf have to be rewarded. The total weekly wage bill for my scouts is about £80. They do not expect big money, providing what they do receive is regular.

I encourage them to be selective and discerning. I would rather them contact me once a month with a really sound proposition, than telephone me every day with news of moderate stuff. This only blurs my vision, rather than clearing it, which is working against the purpose of having scouts. So each week the £80 is divided probably among only a handful of my team of what might be termed 'researchers'. They are my backroom boys who give me daily reports. Sometimes three of them will tell me that they have 'certainties' all running in the same race. This is when one's own judgment is so vital. One has to assess not only the horses but also the form of the scouts who have given the tips. For example, 'Big Bill' from Beckhampton may tend to exaggerate, but 'No Lies Joe' from Epsom you know is never wrong when he says 'this is Coronation Day, celebrate man, celebrate.'

Often, though, when there is good information about several horses in the same race, the right answer is no bet at all. Yes, you pay for not even having a run for your money. It is far better to pay £20 not to have a wager than £100 on a bet and find yourself on the wrong one.

Breakfast for me is always in Continental tradition. After it has been fully digested, I start to get dressed, always in clothes that become the sport of kings. I spend a considerable amount of time over this necessary chore, ensuring that I am immaculately turned out. The regulation amount of cuff must be showing beneath the sleeve, and every article must be blended together to produce a perfect peacock. This is all part of building up one's self-confidence. Ninety-nine per cent of being a success is looking successful. A man who is poor but feels rich always has a chance. A man who is penniless and feels it, is a non-starter.

I make a point always of being one of the first arrivals at the course, because it is the early bird that catches the worm. During the drive to the track, I sit quietly in the back of the Rolls making a final appraisal of the form. By the time I reach the course, I know what every horse, jockey, trainer and owner had for breakfast. What is more important, I know which horses left their breakfast and which ones went up for a second helping. Despite having absorbed all that information, I still have an open mind when I walk on to the track.

Most of the 'regulars' gather near the paddock before the first race. I pass the time of day with most of them and perhaps even compare notes. All the time I am looking and listening. While my eyes are focused on the horses exercising in the paddock, my ears are picking up every nearby conversation. If you notice a trainer or a jockey involved in an intense and somewhat furtive discussion outside the weighing room, or anywhere near the paddock, check the direction of the wind and move into a position where you can hear as much as possible without revealing that you are 'bugging' the conversation. The best way of eavesdropping in this situation is to pretend to be studying the racecard and to keep looking away from where the little *tête-a-tête* is taking place.

I once heard a trainer say to a jockey, who was riding his one runner of the afternoon, 'there is only one danger to us in the whole race.' The wind must have suddenly changed direction because I missed the name of the horse which the trainer believed was the only threat. However, it was enough for me to glean that one trainer was certain that his jockey was taking part in a two-horse race, which was of considerable help considering that there were sixteen runners in the field. This particular trainer's horse had an obvious chance, but form can be like an iceberg, with most of it concealed under the surface. A horse can run ten times, never reaching a place, and yet be a 'good thing' in its eleventh race because it has been dropped in class. The horse on this occasion was a 100-8 chance. I backed it win and place on the Tote. In a grim finish it was beaten into second place, but the Tote paid 4-1 a place. In reality, although beaten, I had backed a 4-1 winner. The actual winner was returned at 20-1, so I doubt whether that was the horse the trainer of the second had believed to be the only danger. The sudden change of wind on that occasion probably saved me money.

You cannot afford to ignore anyone on the race-course. The giggly girl with the beatnik boyfriend may be the daughter of a famous trainer. And the outraged trainer, desperate to get rid of his offensive offspring and her long-haired layabout, probably has given them the biggest certainty of the year to provide enough money for them to emigrate to Venus. Before the heat is on, I have a leisurely lunch on the course. I may have a cool lager with the meal, but that is the last drink I have until racing is over for the day. Gambling, like most other trades, cannot be done efficiently on an empty stomach.

Some of the contacts I have spoken to on the telephone earlier in the day before I left home, may be at the races. If they are, I check with them to ensure that nothing has changed. If it transpires one of them has given me a winner, I tell him what a clever boy he is, stick a glass of champagne in one of his hands, a few 'readies' in the other, and instruct him to keep up the good work so that The Butterfly can continue flying in the manner to which he is accustomed. During the racing I go through the ritual which I outlined in the chapter on the principles of betting at the track.

Many days I do not have a bet, but I might well note half a dozen horses that will win at the next attempt. I call this a long-term investment. Most people *must* gamble if they are on the racecourse or in the betting shop. They would feel cheated, rather like a deprived child, if they went away without having a gamble. The majority of punters feel that they must go home with their pockets either bulging or busted. In their eyes, to leave the course without having dug deep is like a knight who has failed to draw his sword. So they have to bet to satisfy their pride and honour. Rash courage in this game can be very costly. I prefer to be a wealthy coward.

The moment I walk off the course, I buy an evening paper and turn to the following day's race card. My chauffeur knows better than to ask questions about the day's sport. Her job is to look pretty and drive, in that order. Occasionally she keeps me amused with some scintillating chat, but never when I am studying form, racing form, of course!

The majority of racegoers retire to the bars after the last event to hold post-mortems. Most of them bore each other, and themselves, bleating about how they were robbed. It would be a great contest between the racing and soccer fan to see which is the more prejudiced and partisan. I've got a feeling I know where my money would go. . . . While the inquests move on from the racecourse bars to the pubs, and then to clubs, the winners' winnings are bled away until they are the corpses in need of post-mortems. Believe me, they, maybe you, are dead dumb. What the winners have won on the roundabout course, they lose on a swinging club. The only difference between the winners and the losers is that the first named have more to lose.

The regular backer should always keep proper books, with every item and expenses listed. This does not only include bets, but every penny spent in the pursuit of the sport. People forget the money laid out in entrance fees, on newspapers, racecards, train tickets and drinks. Every racegoer is about £10 down before placing a single bet. A man puts a pound on a 10-1 winner and he kids himself that he has won himself a 'tenner'. He has done no such thing. He has just recovered the outlay for the privilege of playing the game. You are competing for profit only the moment all the day's expenses have been regained.

As soon as I arrive home I soak for an hour in a big bubbly bath, just relaxing and contemplating the evening's *sport*. This is the time to relax and unwind in luxury. After a marathon soaking, out comes the night gear. I select my suits according to my mood and for cufflinks I use blondes. Mind you, girl friends who are heavy on the arm do not last long with The Butterfly; they are bad for the sleeve creases. Mostly I dine somewhere in Mayfair, usually at one of the pricey 'in' joints which impress the ladies, and keeps my image intact, if only with myself. Remember, Jack is a very important person to flatter. When times are bad it is necessary that there should be someone, somewhere who believes in you. My philosophy is never to trust anyone else. You cannot afford to in my particular game. So when you are in the rough, on the golf course or in life in general, the best person to have on your side is Jack - occasionally Jill can help a little, of course! I don't like to become too introspective in case I come across something I don't like, so back to that ancient sport of dining and wining. While the little ladies – I use the word 'ladies' only as an opposite to 'men' – devour the atmosphere and the company, I concentrate on demolishing a flaming steak with all the tasty trimmings.

Snap decisions are essential for anyone who is going to survive in the bizarre world of gambling, whether it is on the racecourse or in the casino. One becomes conditioned to making split-second assessments and demands. Gradually this becomes part of one's make-up and character, and is no longer just switched on when walking on a racecourse and turned off when leaving. For the good or bad, I find myself making these crisp valuations of people. Even in a restaurant, this restlessness is evident. The service must be fast or else I storm out... with my blonde cuff links somewhat ruffled! Speed has become my criterion. Understandably perhaps, when one is relying on racehorses for a living.

After eating in style, I may move on to one of the many night clubs, or casinos, of which I am a member. I know people who make a living out of playing roulette or blackjack, but these games have no attraction for me, mainly because I do not understand them. A roulette wheel, as far as I am concerned, is nothing more than a carousel of corruption. It is sudden death; a spinning wheel, a little white ball rolling in the opposite direction and plop, bang goes your cash.

Some people have systems and night after night walk away from the table with chips between their toes and nose. Some carpenters are good at making chairs, while others are experts at producing cabinets. In other words, every gambler should stick to his own game. Just because one is a gambler, it does not follow that one should bet on every fly running up the wall.

I am a social drinker and while my date enjoys a modest flutter on 'the wheel', I like to remain at the cocktail bar, meeting people and talking about everything serious from horses to harems. Bedtime comes at some hour after night has become morning. The human body does not need much sleep, but I would not miss those sweet dreams for anything. . . .

CHAPTER SIX

Betting Shop Betting

Betting shops have revolutionised racehorse gambling. Today, ninety per cent of the organised and pre-planned horseracing coups in Britain are pulled off in the High Street. There are numerous reasons for this new trend, not the least being the betting tax. On the course, the punter pays one shilling in the pound tax, compared with eightpence in the betting shop. A squabble over fourpence may seem like penny-pinching, but the difference can amount to hundreds of pounds when playing for king-size stakes. Many professional punters, who for years were colourful characters on the racecourse, now conduct their business in the thousands of 'shops' that have started to challenge pubs for a majority. Betting shops have become part of the High Street scene, along with Marks and Spencer, the chemist and the butcher. These 'shops' have sprung up like mushrooms. Beware, though, for some have turned out to be toadstools! There are so many these days that you can afford to be a keen 'shopper'. The housewife who keeps a careful, shrewd eye on her budget does not rush in and buy the first cabbage she sees. She compares the quality and prices of goods in several places before making a purchase. The punter must do the same where betting shops are concerned.

Never place a wager in a 'shop' until you have read the rules, especially those in small print, which must be displayed prominently somewhere on the premises – and that does not mean in bold letters in the private 'not for the customers' use' lavatory. All the 'shops' have their own rules, but those belonging to the giant organisations usually give the punter the fairest deal. You should search for a bookmaker who is operating on a 'No Limit' basis. Be on your guard, though, for bookies who proudly boast 'No Limit' in Empire State Building sized letters and then qualify the claim with 'certain' conditions in writing that requires a telescope to be read. These conditions may mean that there is no limit up to a 200-1 double, or 300-1 treble. The Butterfly does not have anything to do with these jokers, and neither should you.

The same bookies do not impose a limit on how much YOU can lose. Oh! boy, no! They are big heroes who are prepared to box with you, providing you promise not to hit them and agree to have your hands tied behind your back. No, my beauties, you need those sick comics like you do mothers-in-law.

In London, there is no problem. There are enough 'shops' belonging to the huge chains where a genuine 'No Limit' is operated. In the Provinces, you may find it necessary to have a number of bookies, using each one for a different sort of bet. One may not accept Tote bets but has no restrictions on all other wagers, and vice versa. Do not walk into the first 'shop' you see and accept, without question, the terms on offer. If you are in a strange town or city, don't leave choosing your punch-bag until a few minutes before the 'off' for the first race. Arrive on the scene early, just as if you were going to the racecourse. The local rules are not the only points that should be considered. There are the seats for example. No self-respecting punter should ever lose money in discomfort. So feel the chairs and make sure the upholstery is to your liking, not too soft, though, because you want to avoid that sinking feeling! Also take into account the atmosphere and decor. A drab and dreary hole in the wall is no place to make you feel good. I know it may be asking the earth, and outer space, too, to expect a bookmaker to smile, but it does help to make winning a little more bearable if the face behind the 'pay-out' grille does not always seem to be accusing you of robbing from a child's piggy bank. Some bookies literally shed tears as they pay out six shillings and ten pence halfpenny, minus tax, of course, to an old age pensioner who has landed a penny each-way accumulator. When it comes to paying out in notes, it is as if the bookie is saying farewell at an airport to some loved one. And when you actually take the notes and stick them in your pocket, that look of disgust and abhorrence is enough to make The Butterfly feel ashamed . . . for not having pinched more!

Some 'shops' can be *too* popular. They become as crowded as a Tube train in London's rush-hour; you know, red-faced city types going even more red when they land in compromising positions with mini-skirted secretaries, and old ladies dying of heart-attacks for being offered a seat by a young gentleman. The only reason I can think of for such crowding in some shops is that the proprietors accept all kinds of bets, except losing ones. An interesting theory, but please do not put it to the test. Bookmakers are many things, but a philanthropist is not one of them.

The type of clientele is also worth considering. Some punters' comments could have been taken from the script of the Al Read Show. You know, the race has been started all of .00001 of a second, and it begins.

'What have you backed? . . . Skint! . . . you must be joking . . . Skint! You soon will be . . . no chance . . . what a jockey! . . . jockey? he couldn't ride a hairwave . . . you don't look that daft . . . how much did you have on it? . . . five bob! . . . you must be loaded . . . why didn't you drop it down the drain? . . . saved you coming 'ere and you'd be home by now . . . do it each way? . . . still no chance . . . you would need to cover the first to last places, then you'd probably still lose . . . no mention of it yet . . . expect it's dead . . . what will the wife say? . . . my advice to you is to stick to bingo . . . '

Across the blower comes, 'And now with a furlong to go it is Skint taking up the running . . . '

To your amazement, Al Read's double starts slapping your back with a paper and yelling, 'Go on Skint, that's my darling boy, go on Skint!' Staggered, you ask, 'What have you backed, then?'

'Skint, of course! Only one 'orse in the race, wasn't there?'

Then there is the other kind, the more vulgar and vitriolic. He starts his tirade at the same time, but continues through the interval between the races. This type is more depressing and irritating. A psychiatrist probably would diagnose a persecution complex. The world is against him, bookmakers, trainers, jockeys, even the horses themselves. It is a monumental conspiracy by the muck and money establishment to deprive the 'ordinary little man' of his dollar.

The dialogue usually goes something like this: 'I knew I shouldn't 'ave backed that b . . . swine of a so-called jockey . . . never mind a dope test, that horse needs a cardiograph to see if it's still alive . . . no use wishing the jockey would break his neck, he couldn't even do that properly . . . that jockey is so bent he steps on his head when he walks ... that 'orse couldn't beat my old woman and she's been dead ten years ....'

When the horse does make its challenge and is beaten in a photograph finish, even the camera is crooked. On he goes, 'We all know it's easy to fix the photograph, don't we? Well, we all know how easy *that* is, don't we? A little touch 'ere and a little touch there ... too much to expect I would win, isn't it? It's the likes of us that keep racing going, but no one fiddles for us, do they?'

When this type does win, then it is a ghastly plot to pacify him so that he will go on squandering his silver. He cannot win and neither can racing. If I go into a 'shop' and discover it is full of 'The Persecuted Ones', I stay the length of time it takes to get out!

Bookmakers' offices are no longer places to be entered furtively, making sure no family friend sees you. All the best people are using them these days. There are the executive 'shops' down in the city, where the customers are dressed in morning suits, all ready for *mourning* their luck, no doubt. Doctors in Harley Street have their own 'local', where they can nip in between an interesting slipped disc and an ugly cyst. Lawyers, too, have their place for a spot of fun during a change of briefs! Housewives, who used to meet to exchange local scandal in the Ye Olde Tea Shop, now do it over the *Sporting Life* in Ye Moderne Betting Shop. And who better than women to know all about a good nag! An example of the kind of confidential get-together you hear is: 'You know my next door neighbour, Mabel? Well, only yesterday morning I saw a pair of black pyjamas on her line ...'

'Fancy her wearing black pyjamas ...'

'She doesn't wear pyjamas, her husband does ...'

'What's funny about that?'

'That's the point, he doesn't have a pair of black pyjamas . . . '

'How do you know?'

'I've seen all his collection by now, haven't I?'

'Perhaps he's got a new pair . . . '

'Don't be silly, there's no holes in the others yet!'

'So that means . . . '

'Talking of colours, Lord Derby's racing silks are black and white, so that in itself must be a tip . . . '

And so it goes on, all charming, wholesome, dirty gossip.

In a betting shop a punter can be at Kempton Park, Newmarket, Ripon and Ayr all in one afternoon. He can relax in sumptuous surroundings with all the racing newspapers at his disposal, free of charge. He does not even have to risk pulling a muscle turning over the general news pages to get at the racecards.

All that is done for him by the bookmaker's mate who pins up the racing pages until it looks as if the place is a printers' parlour.

In many ways, I feel as if I am back at school when I walk into a betting shop. There in front of me is a huge blackboard. Everyone is looking at the blackboard, which is the main difference between a classroom and a betting shop. Some young fellow, who could be a student teacher except that he gets wages, is frantically scratching away with a rapidly disintegrating stick of chalk. On that board is recorded every scrap of market information which has been communicated within seconds from the course. Every time there is a betting change on the track, it is flashed back to all the betting shops throughout Britain.

The good bookmakers will also inform their customers of last-minute jockey changes, the draw for each race and any alterations in the advertised going.

In fact, you are almost told of every occasion a horse or a jockey sneezes on the way to the post. The only information not given is when a horse is wearing blinkers. The sooner all bookmakers provide information about horses wearing blinkers, the better. As I have already stated, horses in blinkers for the first time are usually a good proposition.

Keep your eyes fixed on the blackboard. All the answers are there, staring at you all in lilywhite letters. The punter in the betting shop, in many ways, is in a more advantageous position than his counterpart on the course. This is because each 'shop' is like a computer in which every bit of information is assimilated and then is fed to the customer in an easily comprehensible form. On the track, the punter has to flit from one bookmaker to another all the way along the ring and down the rails if he is to get an overall picture of the transactions taking place. Also, in the 'shop' there is none of the frenetic atmosphere of the course. You can wait and watch dispassionately in the air of cool detachment while all the financial dealings on the track are relayed back.

The rules for on-course betting should be applied in the 'shop'. If you believe that you have 'sussed' out a blot on the handicap, always snap up the first price available before the torrential downpour of money on the course saturates the market. This way you are still beating the book, although many miles away from all the action.

Make your betting plans long before the actual battle commences. Like on the battlefield, if you make a mistake you must expect to fall with it. It is no use a soldier asking for his head back after it has been blown off. Likewise, once the punter parts with his money it is an irrevocable step. Therefore he must have a clear head during every minute of the action. To achieve this clarity of thought, the punter must have decided early in the day in which race, or races, he is going to be interested.

Sudden death strikes the chap who rushes into a betting shop thirty seconds before the 'off', sees that a horse has been backed down from 10-1 to 9-2 and dashes to the counter, scribbling out a bet on the way and having his wager accepted just as the 'blower' commentator is saying 'off at Sandown 3.31.' This is one of the most common and tragic scenes in betting shops. He has not given himself time to look at the 'card' and to observe that the animal for which all the money is flooding is giving Lester Piggott a lift. He was too late arriving to be able to analyse the earlier results and see that Piggott already had ridden two winners. Just a brief, reasoned appraisal of the situation would have shown him that the market move for this horse was a false one, being caused by all the trebles and yankees running on Piggott's third mount. This punter beat himself. This is the bookmaker's secret weapon. The bookie, remember, although your enemy, is a non-participator in the war. He is like a coconut on a stick at the fair, just stuck up to have things thrown at him. Like the man with the coconut stall, the bookie is gambling on you missing. You are the one who makes the mistakes. If you pick nothing else but winners, there is not a thing in the world the bookmaker can do to stop your run. The coconut man is helpless against the thrower who is never off target. Both the bookie and the fairground man make a living out of people who miss many more times than they hit. In other words, avoiding the losers is more important in gambling than being able to find winners.

If you start from the bottom, deciding in your own

opinion, which horses in a race *cannot* possibly win, then you are on the way to discovering which one *will* win. So sort yourself a pleasant quiet corner in your favourite 'shop', go through all the 'cards', putting a great, thick black line through all large handicaps. Confine your business to medium-sized two-year-old fields and three-year-old stakes races, unless in one of the handicaps you have unearthed a real 'blot'. If you believe that the handicapper has slipped up, check, re-check and check again before you support your belief with real money.

You may be an expert decorator. The handicapper is an expert on horses' form. You make very few mistakes in your job. I can assure you that the handicapper is almost always beyond reproach in his vocation. Many people have lost fortunes thinking that the handicapper had slipped up. There is also a racing saying, and a very true one, that 'Someone up There must love him', because when a mistake has been made, incidents often occur during the race to level up the scales. However, if after all re-examinations you are still convinced, then follow your nose and the scent all the way to the hidden treasure.

Leave selling races well alone, unless you see what appears to be a genuine gamble on a horse trained by Ingham, Todd, W. Marshall, especially over hurdles, or J. Sutcliffe, Jnr. Marshall and Sutcliffe are specialists at that type of race and they make a mistake as often as Leap Year comes around.

Condition races are another safe gambling medium. So always make a point of reading the black print above the list of runners in the newspapers. The conditions of each race are explained in bold type, as if begging people to read the special stipulations. For example, the conditions of a race may be that it is for three-year-olds who have not won since the previous season. In such a race the previous year's champion two-year-old could be getting weight from inferior animals just because they had run and won as three-year-olds, whereas the classic horse had not been out that season.

The age of the betting shop has brought about a healthy simplification in the organisation of the big-time coups. The action can be spread all over a city, a county or a country. It is mileage that now maketh millionaires, walking from one 'shop' to another, quietly and unobtrusively spreading the money around so that no one bookmaker stands to finish up in the poor house. This way none of the money gets back to the course, the price is not murdered and everyone is happy.

In the old days, it had to be all subterfuge and skulduggery. There was so much cloak and dagger routine that race meetings could have been mistaken for a convention of secret agents. This attitude was necessary because all the money had to be invested on the course, therefore the punter in The Butterfly's class, who knew a thing or two, had to try to lure bookmakers into offering ridiculously high odds about a horse which should really be favourite. This was achieved by spreading rumours that the animal was not right, or the jockey was taking a 'dive', but some time during the proceedings your true hand had to be shown – when the money had to go down.

Bookmakers, like elephants, never forget. The same trick could never be played twice. Many punters spend so much time dreaming up fantastic, bookie-beating ruses they did not have any time left to study racing. They ended up with plenty of ideas, but no horses.

Now the professional punter does not have to worry

The Butterfly will follow a horse around the world.
Here he is in Belgium to back a winner

Above: The Butterfly
compares notes at
Kempton Park.
Left: The Butterfly
plays hard . . . even
when it comes to
relaxing

so much about gimmicks. All he needs to do is keep on walking, being very democratic by spreading the suffering among a lot of bookmakers instead of confining the misery just to a few. Once I started touring betting shops to back one horse three days before it was due to run. By the time I had finished there were giant holes in my shoes, pockets and bank balance. A few minutes later I could have bought a shoe shop, a men's outfitters and my own bank. The horse, appropriately enough, was called Hopeful Venture!

F

CHAPTER SEVEN

Bedtime Stories

I was never one of those kids who went wild about Humpty-Dumpty or Cinderella. No matter how hard my mother tried, I could not get 'hooked' on those 'And they lived happily ever after' fairy tales. The only kind of bedtime story that was guaranteed to knock out me for the night would be about four-legged heroes. My tastes have not changed. I can listen to racing stories day and night, eight days a week and thirteen months a year. Some people like to recite poetry. To me, racing stories *are* poetry. I am addicted to them. So are most people who have racing in their veins. If I were without a supply of tales of the turf, I would be as lost and desolate as the junkie who could not get a fix. I would be a flat battery, lifeless, no current or spark. Every time I am on the racecourse I am recharged with stories. In some of them I am the central character, sometimes as the monkey, more often the fox.

Most stories that do the circuit are true. Nearly all of them are about big winners, big losers or just big heads. The moral in many of them is that even the immoral come unstuck. Yes, even the fiddles fail sometimes.

What chance has an honest gent like The Butterfly, you may ask? The answer, if the stories are an indication, is about the same chance as the crooks. So make yourself comfortable, caress the hot-water bottle, whatever kind you use! Take a sip of hot milk. Save the sleeping tablets for your mother-in-law. Who cares if Humpty-Dumpty cannot be put together again? Here we go with a few *real* bedtime stories. If you are wise, you will learn something from them. If you are not, well, you will not have read this far. You will be in the bingo hall, waiting for your number to come up, waiting to die.

There were only four runners declared for the 1965 Jockey Club Stakes at Newmarket. Any student of form would not have taken all night to realise that it was really only a two-horse race. The two principals were Baldric II, trained in France and to be ridden by Bill Pyers, and the Newmarket-based Le Pirate. There was also another French-trained horse in the field, called Bal Masque, if four runners can be termed a 'field'. Bal Masque hailed from the same yard as the champion Baldric and was nothing more than the stable hack. Le Pirate was a good old stayer of trainer Thomson Jones, but for me Baldric was a deep freeze certainty. I had kept this one in cold storage for weeks, just waiting to make a pig of myself on the big feast day.

I arrived at Newmarket nice and early, only to discover that Baldric had been withdrawn, leaving just three runners. Along with all the other smart, clever types, I assumed that Baldric's stable companion would take its chance because, even if it had to stop three or four times for breath on the way, it could still not finish any worse than third, for which there was a £200 prize. It also meant that it was now just a one-horse race. Le Pirate replaced Baldric as the certainty.

A boy was due to ride Bal Masque, but just before the race it was announced that Pyers, the Australian

who is based in France, would take over the mount.
There was nothing significant in this move. Pyers, the
stable's number one rider, had come over to partner
the champion and now that Baldric was not taking
part, it seemed obvious that Bill would want to have a
'spin' on the other, just so that he had not travelled
all those miles entirely for nothing.

Bal Masque had not raced for three years and had
never gone beyond six furlongs in public. The Jockey
Club Stakes is run over one and a half testing miles of
undulating going. It was even more of a joke to the
shrewdies like The Butterfly when this camel opened
up an even-money favourite.

I went down to the paddock just to check them over
and Bal Masque had not even been clipped for the
race. It looked something like a cross between a
neglected Highland pony and an un-cut, giant poodle.
I chuckled to myself. So did the others in the big-time.

Gradually, even the general racing public realised
what day it was and punched away on Le Pirate with
the rest of us. Consequently, Bal Masque drifted in the
market like a raft in a flood tide until it was 6-1
against – from evens.

I got myself perched up in the Gods and watched
with a smug smile all across my pretty face as this
French tramp jumped off from the barrier as if in a
five-furlong dash, first one back gets the beans. They
came round into the straight and Bal Masque was still
leading.

'Just watch this thing fold up and die now,' I said
to one of my fellow professionals standing beside me.

'It's got so much hair flapping about like wings I
think it's going to take off,' he replied.

We laughed, feeling warm and good inside at the
knowledge that at any moment Le Pirate was going to

strike the front and run away up the hill, breaking the heart of the French invader from across the Channel. At the 'bushes' it was still Bal Masque setting a cracking gallop, and when it was still leading at the dip before the final furlong in rising ground, my heart momentarily faltered, but quickly I pulled myself together. Miracles of this magnitude may happen in the Bible, but not on the racecourse, I reassured myself. Seconds later, Bal Masque was flashing past the winning post, with the other two straddled behind.

I went downstairs for some fresh air, while the 'mugs' went to collect their money. Later, a friend said to me: 'I love this sport, the trouble is I've got to keep finding money for it!'

One of my biggest wins was on Sea Bird II in the English Derby. I made something in the region of £23,000 and I rate that colt the most sensational of this century. From my London flat, I followed Sea Bird's progress in France as if it were a 'pop' star and I were the agent. I have a scout in France who is in my pay, and he was giving me daily reports on the development of this fantastic colt.

The reports were so encouraging that I decided to take a trip over to France and look at him for myself. I wanted to make sure that there was no question of exaggeration. It is better to underrate the capability of a horse than to overestimate. Somebody who lives with anyone every day tends to become attached and too close to the subject to be objective. That is like a parent, who is the worst judge of his or her child's ability. I wanted to be positive that my French scout had not become too devoted to the 'Bird'. A detached view and a second expert opinion was imperative. So I crossed the Channel to watch Sea Bird in its first race as a three-year-old. The colt did everything asked of him and trotted in effortlessly. It was not so much the win, but the amount it had in reserve that impressed me. Later that April, it gained another painless victory. According to the reports I was receiving, he was making rapid improvement by the hour. Nothing in the stable could live with him. By early in May, I was convinced that nothing in the world would ever see anything more than the tail of this wonder horse. There was one obstacle. At this stage Sea Bird was not earmarked for the English Derby.

Then one morning that May the colt's connections, after a private conference with trainer Polet, declared that Sea Bird would come to Epsom. It was meant to be the most closely-guarded secret in racing. Less than an hour after that decision had been taken, the phone was ringing in my West End home. It was my contact man, an Australian, calling from Chantilly.

'I'm sure you won't mind my transferring the charge today,' he said crisply.

'At your service,' I replied. 'Speak up though. I don't want anything to have to be repeated at GPO prices.'

The secret was out. Sea Bird was to run in the English Derby.

'Get off the line,' I shouted. 'I've got to ring up a bookie and order myself a fortune.'

This, to me, was the bet of the century. I telephoned William Hill and asked, 'What price Sea Bird for the Derby?' When the reply was 8-1, I knew that I was ahead of the punting field. I must have been the only person in Britain at that moment who knew of the change of plans. My bet that morning was to win £10,000. By the following day the Press had caught up with the news and immediately all the national bookmakers slashed the odds from 8-1 down to 4-1.

I continued to back the beautiful 'Bird' with every bit of bread and butter money I made from day-to-day betting. I even cut down on the style of the cuff links I wore at playtime so that I could lay out more on the only 'Bird' of real class in my life at that time. I lived really rough, sometimes struggling through on only one steak, instead of two, a day, or perhaps buying only one new suit a week. You can see, I am able to live spartan when it is necessary!

On the day, the 'Bird' started 7-4 favourite and like a true champion he had the race won by Tattenham Corner, landing me a net profit of £23,000. I had roughed it to such an extent in the weeks before the Derby that when it was all over I decided that I was entitled to a holiday. So I booked myself on a three and a half months trip around the world, visiting twenty-two countries. I left England on the *Queen Mary* for New York and the rest of my world tour was continued by air. It was a tour of all historic places. I visited the oldest bars in the world! Strangely, most pleasure was derived from the silence and solitude of being away from everything. No telephones ringing, no screaming bookmakers, no nagging cuff links!

There is another story concerning Sea Bird. The colt went on to run away with the Arc de Triomphe with the most comfortable and casual victory in the history of this famous race. The jockey was Pat Glennon, another Australian. After coming in to one of the most tumultuous welcomes given to a rider, Pat threw down his saddle and said, 'I'm finished.'

It was the culmination of twenty years' hard work and honest endeavour. He had suffered weight problems and he needed to waste almost every day. At the height of his career, suddenly he became sick of everything and everyone. While people were still applauding him, Pat was hanging up his boots for ever. Nobody believed him at the time. I knew Pat well and when I saw the look on his face I had no doubts that he would never ride again. He received lucrative offers to ride in America, but turned down them all. In the best tradition of the entertainment business, he retired while at the top. Now, he lives simply and humbly in Adelaide.

The art of punting is to play it race by race until you think that you have discovered a champion. When that day does come, follow the animal to the end of the earth. I followed Sea Bird and he led me to gold.

Now I shall tell you about a 'Dash for Cash'. This takes place in California where they have the fastest horses in the world competing for the highest prize money in the world, over the shortest distance in the world.

For an international racegoer like myself who was broken in with bush racing in the outback of Western Queensland, where I cut my teeth, and emigrated to savour the satisfying pleasure one gets on a sunny day in the garden atmosphere of British racing, this quarter horse racing of California was remarkable. I was astounded to see those ponies flash over short distances at such speed. I was amazed to find that the world's richest horse race is run under these rules.

Just think, £94,950 goes to the winner of a 400-yard 'Dash for Cash', at Ruidoso Downs, in the State of New Mexico, every Labour Day, which in the USA is the first Monday in September. All runners share a purse to the value of £202,325. These staggering figures make the marathon staying test of an Ascot Gold Cup over two miles and six furlongs, and worth only £8,400 to the winner, seem just an egg and spoon race.

Quarter racing was founded by the early colonials in the eastern states, as far back as 1609 and, as they had very little cleared land, they used to have local match races down the main street of the town or village. This was a very popular sport for all, especially on Sunday after church, when they would have the weekly race, the result being the town's topic of conversation for the next week. Then, as the vast nation spread west so did the pony racing, but even when it reached the plains west of the Mississippi they still kept the weekly racing confined to the main street. So over the centuries the races have always been two furlongs, until recent years when they have been staged over 400 yards.

At the turn of the century, the breed was officially called, 'The Celebrated American Quarter Horse', and their ancestors are traced back to the Scottish Galloways and Cannemara ponies of the early settlers who crossed these animals with the remnants of the horses left by the Spanish missions in Florida and Georgia. But this breed has already been perfected over the last forty years and huge prices are now obtained for top stallions for breeding. This 'super breed of ponies', as they are called, were once described by an American historian in the following manner . . . 'they race over tiny distances on one, or at most two, breaths. As the race times will indicate, everything happens so quickly that they literally have no time to breathe normally.'

Yes, for backers who like sudden death this is the sport. It nearly always ends in a photograph finish. At least four or five finish within the length of the winner.

I attended a nine-event programme of the Los Alimatos Race Club, which is twenty-five miles due south of Los Angeles in what is known as Orange Country. In every facet, it was like a miniature meeting of Kempton Park with the races run over a distance just short of two furlongs of the straight proper. The track has a dirt surface and starting stalls operate so each event is run in just over twenty seconds. The track record is 19.9 seconds.

One particular race I saw was the sixth running of the Los Alimatos Futurity and the purse was worth £56,300. Every one of the runners received a share of the prize money, the winner took forty-five per cent, the second seventeen per cent, the third ten per cent, and the rest of the cash was divided on a sliding scale. The runner that came in last received £500. This dividing up of the purse is very fair and everyone gets something. The scale of weights is between eight stone and nine stone seven pounds. They also have two-year-old races over 350 yards as well. The older horses are graded into five different classes.

Quarter horse racing at Los Alimatos began in 1951, when the Californian Racing Board made it legal to have pari mutuel betting on this sport and since then it has ascended to great heights. They get large attendances six days a week during the season, and in 1968, for the first time, they raced at night.

This is a happy and modern, thriving sport with a trade mark of its very own, for like the grey topper and black tails seen on the lawn at Royal Ascot, here at Los Alimatos they wear the grey, curled-brim stetson hat, plus the long, colourful embroidered Texas riding boots.

Yes, as I said, a happy and modern thriving sport and I cannot but see that it will continue to attain even greater popularity.

There was one Australian bush trainer who was reduced to one horse. He literally loved this horse and he came to look upon it as his son. Although it had never won a race, he was a proud father. It was a handsome black colt and he groomed it to perfection. Whenever it appeared on a racecourse, it was fitted with a sparkling white bridle and the trainer would lead it around the paddock, talking to it like an anxious parent before his son was about to take part in a school sports meeting. The trainer wanted his charge to be recognised as the best-looking maiden in the country. He was literally afraid that one day it would win a race and therefore lose its maiden status.

All this trainer wanted was for his 'loved one' to capture the scene every time it was on parade before a race. He knew that if it ever won and was up-graded, it would have to compete against better class horses. He feared that his mule would be overshadowed and this he could not face. This trainer travelled all over the country with his horse, racing it at every meeting he could find. And race after race the good-looking maiden finished second.

Everybody was waiting for the jockey to make a mistake one day and win! It seemed that the day for it to cease to be a maiden had arrived when it was the odds-on favourite in a two-horse race at Mingila. I was at the course that day and it was inconceivable that this arrogant animal could get beaten, however much the trainer wanted it to lose. The other 'thing' in the race was a kangaroo that had forgotten how to jump. As the trainer led the horse around the ring, I leaned over the rail and called out mockingly, 'Do you fancy him today?' The trainer replied dead pan out of the corner of his mouth, 'He can't win today, he's got the worst draw in the field!' As I have said, there were two runners. . . .

One day the connections of the very useful Bally-maris decided that they would like Bill Pyers to ride their horse in an important race at York. The horse, trained up north by 'Snowy' Gray, had always been ridden by stable jockey Brian Connorton. When Bill arrived at the Yorkshire track it was the first time in his life that he had set his experienced eyes on Ballymaris. The horse had a reputation of being an individualist, temperamental and strong willed. Even those who rode Ballymaris in home training gallops every morning could never be sure how he would behave. He needed patience and perseverance. What was more important, he did not take kindly to strangers.

There were two short-priced horses in the race and Ballymaris was on offer at 10-1. I knew all about Ballymaris' potential from one of my northern scouts and the fact that Bill had been hired to come all the way over from France was enough for me. After Bill had been given final instructions and was safely on board, the travelling head lad led him out of the paddock. Just before they were on the course, the lad looked up at Bill and said, 'I don't know why they bothered to bring you over. You have got to get to know everything about this horse before he can be ridden.'

Bill replied laconically, 'I've just met him and by the time we've gone past the post together first he'll be one of my best pals!'

Ten minutes later Bill, smiling broadly, was patting his best pal on the neck – as they were steered into the winners' enclosure. I was smiling, too. It is not every day that one backs a 10-1 winner.

Now about one of those fiddles that failed. This was a six-furlong sprint. There were only six runners in the field and two of them were without a chance on the book. All the jockeys in this particular race were in the proposed coup. It was going to be a really big one, running into something in the region of a quarter of a million pounds. The best known of the jockeys in the race was on the horse that was going to be allowed to win. It was expected that this horse would be about third or fourth best in the market on the course. The big boys behind the plot were arranging for the money to be placed later off the course so that the starting price would not be wrecked. The two joint favourites were being 'stopped' and nothing could go wrong. Everything had been taken care of.

Just as they were approaching the final furlong, the horse which was meant to win, took the lead and looked all set to come clear. Then suddenly a little brown stallion, the extreme outsider, wondering what on earth his dozy jockey was doing, decided his pride and honour were worth more than any rider's illicit gains. The little stallion burst through and came with a flying late run. The jockey could not do anything except sit and pray that the challenge was too late. If he tried to 'stop' his mount, he knew that he would be warned off for life because by now they were right under the noses of the stewards.

The jockey on the leader, seeing the danger, raised his whip and, instead of cracking his own mount, brought it down across the nose of the little outsider. Normally, this would have caused enough distress to a horse to prevent it from having any chance. On this occasion, however, the outcome was the reverse. The little stallion, instead of stopping, lunged for the line in anger and got up to win by a short head, as the photograph proved. There have never been so many red faces in the changing room at one time.

Funnily, one of my most satisfying coups was all a horrible mistake. It was at Royal Ascot and there was a considerable amount of information about several horses in one race. I was hopping around the ring like a frog with blisters on its toes trying to see if there was any firm trend in the market transactions. Finally, I made my decision as the large field was lining up at the barrier. It had to be Weeper's Boy, I decided.

I checked the jockeys' list and saw that Stan Clayton was 'up' on Weeper's Boy. Now, as I pointed out in the chapter on jockeys, Clayton is always fabulous value on the Tote. I ran underneath the 'stand to the Tote windows. There was a queue and I was frantic that I would not get my bet on before the 'off'. The bell for the grilles to be shut was just sounding as I reached the window where £1 tickets were sold.

'Fifty tickets to win and one hundred for a place on number six,' I shouted. I was the last one to be served. As I was walking away, 'Long Larry' came up to me and said, 'What have you done, Butterfly?'

'Number six, Weeper's Boy,' I replied.

'What are you talking about. Number six is Foxford Boy. Have you gone crazy? What sort of chance has that snail got?'

You could have lit a cigarette on my cheeks. In the hurry, I had backed the wrong 'boy', or so I thought. By the time I reached the top of the 'stand, the race was just finishing. I did not see a thing. All I heard was the commentator say, 'first number six, Foxford Boy...'

The Tote paid odds of 14-1 a win and 5-1 a place. In other words, I won £700 for the win and £500 for the place – all because I made a ghastly mistake!

On one trip to the Ayr Gold Cup I was very impressed with a midget two-year-old in a small race on the same card as the big event. It looked more like a freak than a racehorse, but the way it glided away from the pack, Wow! As I reclined in the back of the

Rolls on the long journey back from the kilt country, only one thought occupied my mind. I was not concerned with memories of the drama and glamour of the major event of the day. All I could think about was that underdeveloped, grey dwarf. I could not forget the way it accelerated when asked, pulverising the opposition within a couple of dynamic strides.

World-beaters, I knew by experience, did not always look pretty. Just because you win a beauty contest, it does not mean that those well-shaped legs can move faster than all the others. Likewise, the ugly fellows do not automatically have the slowest feet. After all, they have to move the quickest to catch up with the fillies who are fleeing out of fright. Somehow I sensed that beneath the untidy exterior of this little fellow was hidden a power station. It was as if he were bursting at the seams with energy, so far untapped, but just waiting to be unleashed. They called him Althrey Don. So far he was just a joke. He was to become a legend, but very few people on that day could have predicted a champion's future for the 'Don'. One man did, however. And he was prepared to speculate, not just in talk, but in 'readies'. The man with such great faith was yours truly. I worked out that if the 'Don' made the normal sort of progress through the winter and matured, he would go very close to becoming Britain's champion sprinter.

By the early spring of the following season, I had one of my experienced scouts in the north making a daily check on trainer Pat Rohan's young prodigy. His reports were of tremendous encouragement to me. He confirmed that the 'Don' had wintered well and had made satisfactory progress. Althrey Don eventually had his first run in public as a three-year-old in a very small field. He was made the odds-on favourite and

failed to start, whipping round at the start. Immediately, the 'Don' was marked as a 'barrier bandit!' I
knew better. My faith was not shaken in the least. He
came out again and behaved like a real blue-blooded
gent, doing enough but not revealing too much. Now
he was all set for the Nunthorpe Stakes at York.

For six weeks, as in the case of Sea Bird in the
English Derby, I backed Althrey Don for the Nunthorpe with every penny I made from my bread and
butter gambling. On the day of the race it was still
possible to get 9-2 about the 'Don'. It was, however,
forced down to 3-1 just before the 'off'. Piggott was
riding the favourite, Matatina. Only in the case of Sea
Bird have I been sure about a result. So confident was
I that I turned bookmaker and laid Piggott's mount.
If Piggott had won, it would have been a double
defeat for The Butterfly. I would have lost everything
I had laid out on the 'Don' and then have had to pay
all those who had backed Matatina with me. Instead,
it was a double victory for me. The 'Don' beat Piggott's
mount into second place and I cleaned up a not to be
sneezed at £18,000.

This result gave me enormous satisfaction, and not
only from the financial aspect. More than a year
earlier I had seen a little grey baby win a minute race
at Ayr and I had said to myself, 'There is tomorrow's
champion.' This is the way to make a fortune in racing,
discovering winners twelve months in advance.

After the Craven meeting at Newmarket in 1967, I
christened Ribocco 'the little fat pig'. On the way
home I had an even £100 bet with a fellow professional
that Ribocco would not start in the following year's
English Derby, let alone win the most treasured trophy
in racing.

I went to Chester and Lingfield just to wager that

Above: The Butterfly studies tomorrow's card in the back of his Rolls on the way home from the course. *Left:* A Derby Day picnic . . . The Butterfly tucks into chicken salad and his favourite champagne. In the background is the Rolls

The Butterfly takes a stroll in a London Park

'the little fat pig' would *not* win. On both occasions
my money never threatened to leave my pocket. Win!
It had a struggle even to wobble. 'Fatso' had been the
joint winter favourite with Royal Palace for the English
Derby. After performing as well as any pig could be
expected to in the Lingfield Derby trial, it drifted to
50-1 in the ante-post betting market for the major
classic. On Derby Day, though, these odds were
slashed to 20-1. Piggott was riding and already I had
lost my £100 because 'the little fat pig' was a starter.
In fact, on the day Ribocco was one of the best backed
horses in the race. Somebody must have waved a
magic wand over Ribocco if he is going to get into
this race, I said to myself. He ran a superlative race,
finishing second to Royal Palace. I was sure that I had
witnessed the true Ribocco. So I recast my plans. The
professional cannot buy porridge with pride. He must
always be prepared to desert one camp to join the
current winning side.

I went to the Irish Derby just to back the pig and it
obliged, bringing home the bacon! I kept an open
mind for the English St. Leger, but when I saw that
my 'little fat pig' had been transferred into a lovely
limbed racehorse, I stepped in and supported it at all
prices from 6-1 to 5-2. There was never any danger,
Piggott's genius made sure of that.

The Champion Stakes at Newmarket has always
been a good race for me. I was on winners Baldric,
Hula Dancer and Silly Season, just to name a few. The
success of Baldric, though, was a case of mixed
fortunes for me. I had backed Baldric to earn me more
than a month's income. As the race neared the climax
it became more and more apparent that it was develop-
ing into a grim struggle between Baldric and Pieces of
Eight, the latter getting all the help in the world from

G

Piggott. The relentless battle continued all the way up the hill and past the post. I was directly in line with the finish and I had never been more convinced that I was beaten in the very last gasp for breath. Everybody else on the racecourse, including the bookmakers, seemed to agree with my judgment. The bookies were offering 5-1 on and then 6-1 on in the betting on the outcome of the photograph that Pieces of Eight got the lolly.

Desperate to cover myself, I invested heavily on Piggott's mount, even at such long odds on. When the print of the photograph appeared, it showed that Baldric had blown its nose at the right moment and had taken the race by the width of a pimple.

All my 'cover' money had been wasted. Nevertheless, I had still shown a profit on the race, although nothing like the amount if my judgment of the photo finish had been accurate. There is an old saying in racing that the winners can laugh and the losers can please themselves.

One horse which has a place of honour in my hall of memories is that resolute stayer Provoke. Trained by Major Dick Hern, Provoke first entered my note-book of horses to follow after losing the verdict by half a length in a maiden event over a testing mile and a half at Newbury. Its performance that day was one of gameness and dogged determination. In addition, Provoke was superbly bred. I'm afraid even in the animal world to get on depends largely on whom you had for a mum and dad. Provoke, undoubtedly, came out of the most posh drawers.

Being a bit of a snob from the Commonwealth, I believe in following class. So I fell in with Provoke on his next appearance and he won with the arrogance and disdain of a squire seeing off peasants from what he regarded as his heritage. Provoke went on to win at Ascot and York, each time helping The Butterfly to fill his cupboard.

Then came the St. Leger, and I still feel shame for not having had courage to take 33-1 which was on offer. Even after holding such a high opinion of Provoke for so long, when it came to the real crunch I underrated my friend. Somehow I feel that I deserted him that day when he galloped away with the Leger. I had thought the prize a little too rich for him. Nevertheless, it was with the pride of a parent that I cheered Provoke into the winners' enclosure. Yes, I shouted Provoke home, even though I had backed against him!

The year Piggott suffered a serious accident in France, I backed Hutchinson for the British jockey championship. I believed that the 'Happy Horseman' would at last be crowned King of the Saddle, even though the main pretender to the throne was out of action. I should have known better than to allow patriotism to distract my assessment of the situation. Lester came back and in no time at all had re-established himself as the rightful monarch. After this achievement, I was convinced that no one in the world would ever relieve Lester of his title while he was riding full-time.

So the following year, 1967, I put my money on Lester, even while Mercer was setting a roaring pace. Piggott drifted to 6-1 for the championship at one stage when in fourth position. I was asked during an interview on television at Kempton Park for my fancies and I answered, 'Winners are hard to find here, but Piggott is a certainty for the championship.' What a bet when he was 6-1 at the time!

I keep jabbing away at Lester all season, even when

he is 10-1 on, because it is the one bet every year that cannot lose. What I am doing is backing all of Lester's winners in one joint wager.

Sweet Story, trained in the north, was one of Britain's best prospects over a long journey in its day, but it was a barrier rogue and therefore was out as a betting medium for The Butterfly. Sweet Story reminds me of a similar horse in Australia called Fair Rally. This horse refused to start every time it was taken to the barrier. Then the trainer had an ingenious idea. He used it for pulling a cart, not only at his yard but to go into town and to do the shopping. This got Fair Rally accustomed to the enclosed feeling of having something on each side of his flanks. The next season he won five races straight off in a canter.

CHAPTER EIGHT

Television Gambling

The best advice I can give to anyone who likes to have a gamble on races being televised is blow yourself a fuse! Second piece of guidance is fall so far behind with the hire purchase instalments or rental charge that some heavy looking bruiser comes along and carts the set away. You may lose a television set, but probably you lose a lot less in the final balance. The trouble with television coverage is that it restricts you to the races chosen for you by the programme organisers. It may be that the races televised are the large field handicaps which are strictly taboo as far as the professional punter is concerned. You may strongly fancy two horses, but, because they are not running in televised races, you ignore them and look for something on which to have an interest in the event that you are going to be able to watch. All this is making for a very costly afternoon's viewing.

If you must have a bet on televised races, then here are a few hints which will not only contain your losses, but will give you a chance of winning the next instalment or rent on the set.

I'll set the scene for you. It is Saturday afternoon. The lunch has been digested. The coffee looks good and the armchair more inviting. The wife is grooming herself in preparation for going shopping and you cannot slam the door behind her quickly enough. The hours between lunch and tea on a Saturday are by tradition 'stag' time. No woman has the right to encroach upon this 'Men only' world. What self-respecting husband wants his spouse clinging to his arm on the terraces of the local football club as he screams abuse at the referee or hurls bottles at the unprotected head of the opposing team's goalkeeper? Likewise, the racing fanatic does not want his wife asking, 'Do you really like this hat, Albert dear?' while he is slipping off the end of his seat with excitement as 'his' horse hits the front with just a furlong left to run. There is only one place for the wife, girl-friend, fiancée or mistress on a Saturday afternoon, and that is out. As soon as *she* has finished washing up – never, never before – help her on with her coat, tell her how radiant she is looking, try not to lose your tongue in your cheek, and push her off in the direction of the most crowded store where she has the greatest chance of losing herself for the rest of the afternoon. Even if you have to give her a bob or two, it is worth it to prevent women trespassing on man's Saturday sporting scene.

All right, now she has gone. You breathe a sigh of relief, switch on the box, and take out the two cold lagers which you had hidden under the sofa. Make sure that you have something soft on which to rest your feet, and then recline in the armchair, with the television on one side and the lager and cigarettes on the other. When you turn that switch you are whisked away to another world. You are no longer in Britain, Birmingham or Boston. You are at a Cheltenham National Hunt meeting without feeling any of the cold of January frost. You can be at Royal Ascot without being trampled on in the crowds trying to reach the bars, the bookmakers, or just the way out. And if you have 'done' your money, you are spared that sickening

drag of a return journey, tired, feet heavy, pockets
light and spirit scarce. If the results are not to your
liking on one channel, you can always switch over to
another! If it looks as if you are about to be a loser,
you can turn over and forget all about it as you watch
some fat lout being tossed out of a wrestling ring. You
imagine the fellow who has been ejected is your
bookmaker, or the jockey, the trainer, or the horse,
and you discover that you are feeling better already.

I believe that the BBC and ITV provide the most
efficient coverage of racing in the world. I have seen
racing on television in many countries, including
America, and I must compliment the British networks
on the service they provide. It is really first-class.

All the races are expertly covered. You are told the
state of the going, the advantage of the draw, any last-
minute riding changes, the horses wearing blinkers and
those having them fitted for the first time. First-hand
information of the conditions are provided by jockeys
who are interviewed by one of a team of expert
commentators. Trainers and owners are brought
before you, and many speak openly and honestly about
their chances in a race later in the afternoon. You, in
fact, meet the people who have their fingers on the
pulse of racing. And the interviewers put all the
questions you would like to ask if ever you had the
chance to meet these people. But even if Ryan Price is
being questioned and he says, 'I cannot be beaten' in
such and such a race, do not be swayed entirely by his
statement. It is his opinion. You may not share his
view. If you have a reason for not agreeing with him,
then stand by your own judgment, but just look again
very closely at the Price-trained entry to ensure that
there is nothing you have overlooked.

The commentator gives details of each horse and

helps you by pinpointing which ones will be best suited by the going. They also give their fancies and the reasons for their choice. Once again you should listen carefully to what they have to say, without taking their word as gospel. Pick their brains and combine their information with yours. This way you will have a complete insight to the prospects of each horse.

The television screen can flash the viewer to the paddock, the betting ring, the grandstand, the course and the start, all within a matter of seconds. No punter on the course could have such a comprehensive round-up of the entire proceedings. The viewer should take full advantage of this unique service. When the cameras are focused on the horses in the parade ring, follow the instructions I gave in the chapter concerning on-course betting and look for the elegant walkers. Instead of having to stand on stilts to obtain an unobstructed view, the television cameras take you into the ring as if you were an owner or trainer of one of the runners. Strangely, although you may be sitting two hundred miles away from the meeting, it is possible for you to be more involved than the majority of people on the course. Racegoers at Newbury can be more remote and forgotten than the armchair participator at Newcastle. Sitting back there in luxury, with your first half lager gone, you have no difficulty picking out the animals that are sweating up. Most owners like all their relatives and friends to be present when they have a winner, so if you see a rather large party in the ring connected with one horse, it is always worth while paying a little extra attention to that animal's history and immediate future prospects.

By the time the runners are leaving the paddock, most punters at the meeting are making their way to

their favourite bookmaker, or are already looking for
a 'place with a view' in the 'stand. Therefore, if there
is a late crisis in the paddock, very few racegoers are
aware of any such development. A horse that had been
as docile as a henpecked husband suddenly could think
he was entered in the Shrove Tuesday pancake race,
toss the jockey in the air twice, and make off in the
direction of the nearest High Street. Many times I
have been on a course when a race has been delayed
fifteen or twenty minutes, and it is only while reading
the evening papers on the drive home that I learned
the hold-up was due to a horse having to be replated
at the last minute. It is not uncommon for a horse to
spread a plate in the paddock. When there is any
incident of importance, the television camera relays it
to you at home as it is happening. You do not have to
hear about it second, third or twenty-eighth hand. You
are taken to the very spot where it is all happening,
so that you can see for yourself and draw your
own conclusions regarding the significance of the
situation.

When the runners are all out on the course the
television cameras usually provide close-up shots of
each one as they canter down the course to the start.
Watch very carefully and note the smooth, reaching
movers. Those that catch the eye will be, in all
probability, the same ones you noted as attractive
walkers in the paddock. By this stage you should have
drawn up a short list of possibles. Do not commit
yourself finally until you have heard the latest betting
news.

It is a rare occasion if I back a horse at odds of more
than 5-1. The animals I support are usually in the span
between 7-4 and 5-1. This is the area from which
come the vast proportion of winners. If one of the

horses to impress you during the preliminary proceedings is in that betting range, then that is the one
to be on. Perhaps two horses for which you have a
liking quite obviously have been supported substan-
tially in the market. One may be at 6-4, while the other
is 5-1 chance. Now it is all a question of value. In your
opinion, there can be little to choose between them or
you would not have two on your list. The decision
would be clear-cut if any one stood out head and mane
above the others. So my advice is to oppose the
short-priced favourite. Back the 5-1 shot each way. If
you have done your homework properly, it should be
a 'knocking' bet.

If you have a credit account, you can wait until the
very last second before ringing through your bet.
This way you can ensure that the horse you propose to
back has been placed in the starting stalls safely. In
other words, like a security guard, you are protecting
your money all the way from the bookmaker's bank
to your own!

In distance events at Newmarket, Newbury and
Doncaster – to name just a few – the racegoers see no
more than the last three or four furlongs. The rest of
the race takes place out of sight of the 'stands. The
racegoers have only the course commentator's word
for who is leading and who is lagging. Television,
however, takes the viewer through every stride of the
most marathon of British races, including the two and
a half mile Cesarewitch at Newmarket. The racing fan
has never had it so good – providing he stays at home.
It is about time that racecourse officials appreciated the
potential of closed-circuit television. If giant cinema-
scope-sized screens were situated in the 'stands and all
the bars, I am sure the decline in attendance figures
would be checked overnight.

The problem is that British racecourses were built for the horses and not for the spectators. In Australia and America the case is reversed. Newmarket is typical of the traditional British track, straight, long and galloping. When the horses come into view for the first time, they have already been running for 'half an hour'. They appear on the horizon like an approaching hurricane, dust swirling, and the rumbling and thudding increasing in volume with every second. By the time you can actually sort out the colours, the race is over. Even with the best glasses in the world, you cannot see more than the last three furlongs at New-market, the headquarters of British racing, because of the hidden ground caused by the dips and hollows.

Glasses are not needed in Australia or America because all races are on circular courses and about three circuits are required to complete a mile. These tracks have been constructed to appeal to the public, and not just those within the Establishment's inner sanctum. Racing in Australia and America is the sport of workers, the kings sell the hamburgers and the peanuts.

The television viewer is bang on the line and is in a better position than most on the course to judge the outcome of a close finish. Be cautious, though, if you are considering gambling on a photo finish, because the camera angle can be very deceptive on some courses.

Try to avoid becoming a compulsive television gambler. Just because a race is being televised, there is no reason why you must have a financial interest. Only the most self-disciplined characters have any chance of showing a profit consistently. The racing viewer must condition himself so that he is content to watch a whole afternoon's sport without laying out a penny. In fact, he must be as strict with himself as the professional punter on the course.

One of my most rewarding day's work – excuse the bad language, it just slipped out in a brief aberration – came one week-end while I was suffering from a severe cold. I had spent most of the week in bed, coughing, spluttering and generally feeling sorry for myself. By Saturday I had missed half a dozen good things and three swinging parties. This state of affairs could not continue, I told myself. If I was going to die, at least my epitaph was going to be something like 'A hundred each way on Funeral Procession.' So I tottered from my bed and collapsed into a soothing rocking-chair, which, by sheer coincidence, happened to be facing the television. Also by sheer coincidence, it happened to be approaching three-thirty in the afternoon, the time for the major race at Sandown Park. Wrapping a blanket around my shivering body until I looked something like an Egyptian mummy, or an Australian punter covered by a blanket, I switched on and, within seconds, I was among the thronging thousands at that exacting and demanding course at Esher, Surrey. There were so many people at Sandown that day they appeared like germs under a microscope. The thought served only to remind me of my cold, so I stopped thinking. Being uncomplicated has its advantages.

The jockeys were just entering the paddock. I thought that one horse had an outstanding chance, but I was not prepared to support my opinion with money because I knew the odds would be so cramped. The trainer had engaged a French jockey, which was proof that someone else also shared my view. Foreign jockeys do not usually come all the way to Britain just for the ride. They have enough scrubbers in their own country without going overseas to find them. A betting flash appeared on the screen and the horse being partnered by the Frenchman was odds-on.

Now, I was not interested in the race as a betting proposition. Just at that moment the television cameras spotlighted the French jockey. It was obvious that the English trainer was having difficulty in making the French jockey understand the riding instructions. The trainer seemed to be speaking pidgin-English and was gesticulating desperately with his arms. Still the little chappie from East of Calais kept shaking his head and shrugging his shoulders. Finally the trainer pointed to his lips, obviously telling the jockey to observe very closely. By now the camera team had realised that they were capturing an unspoiled piece of spontaneous, situation comedy. Television exploited it to the full. The cameras moved in close. The trainer's frustrated face was near enough for him to catch my cold. The close-up shots were so effective that I was able to lip-read. The trainer was saying 'dormir . . . dormir'. . . . He kept repeating the word, and slapping his backside at the same time. I was sure of the French word he kept saying, but I could not fathom out the meaning of the bottom slapping.

The message the trainer had been frantically trying to impart must have suddenly been conveyed, because the Frenchman started rolling about in an hilarious spasm, rocking with great guffaws and nodding so zealously that he looked like a Moslem praying in the garden of a mosque. No microscope was necessary to reveal that with every nod the jockey was saying, 'Oui monsieur oui monsieur, oui monsieur'.

Not surprisingly, the Frenchman was the last to leave the paddock. The trainer scratched his head all the way to the grandstand, obviously wondering whether in fact he had got through to the '*Je ne parle pas Anglais*' rider. As the horses made their way down to the barrier, I tried to decipher the message passed from the trainer to the jockey in an improvised code. It must have been important, I reasoned with myself, for the trainer to have persevered at the expense of his own embarrassment. The answer dawned on me quite by chance. Just a few minutes earlier I had been reading an article by a racing correspondent in a daily newspaper. The correspondent had criticised a jockey for 'going to sleep' on a mount the previous day. The solution was staring me in the face. '*Dormir*' means to sleep. The slap on the backside was significant. 'Of course!' I exclaimed. 'Go to sleep and stay at the rear of the field.' That was the message.

I picked up the telephone and rang my favourite bookmaker. 'What odds will you lay me the French jockey and his mount in the big 'un don't get placed?' I asked.

There was a brief pause. Then the reply, 'You may have fives Butterfly'. . . .

'I'm on for a hundred,' I replied.

The jockey had a pleasant afternoon's siesta. The trainer must have felt as if he had been in a Turkish bath, but no doubt had more weight off his mind than anywhere else! Me, I was proud of my transaction. The cold, though, had turned into a fever. That is the danger of gambling, it makes high temperatures higher.

Anyway, thank heaven for television.

CHAPTER NINE

Bookmakers

There are two kinds of bookmakers – the bad and the worst. I should know, because I was once one myself, and so was my father. Since I moved to Britain, at least twelve bookmakers have closed my account because I was a regular winner. This would not have happened anywhere else in the world where bookmakers are officially recognised and are permitted to make a living without going underground.

When I first arrived in Britain, the bookies thought I was a rave. They had not seen anything quite so funny since they last cut each other's throat. I laughed with them. After all, I am prepared to share a joke with *anyone*. They had heard that when I opened a bank account I did not ask for an overdraft. Nothing like that had happened in England since the beginning of the new affluence! They were falling over backwards off their banana boxes in the scramble to offer me credit accounts. I was almost overcome by the British hospitality – except I had been a bookmaker myself. The cynic that I might be, for some unaccountable reason I could not clear my mind from the thought that there might be an ulterior motive in all the friendliness. I was even degrading enough to believe that people were after my money! How low and despicable can one become? I was so ashamed of myself that I felt I must accept the kind offers. So I opened a number of accounts and immediately started sparring.

In the first few days I landed one or two knock-outs.
I kept on being friendly, smiling away and laughing
raucously as I collected £1,000 here and £2,000 there.
I could not understand, though, why suddenly I was
the only one smiling! They all started taking me so
seriously, yet I thought it was still all such good fun....

Seriously, though, if bookmakers are not prepared
to accept regular winners on their books, then they
should likewise close the accounts of all the consistent
losers. I am surprised that some credit bookies, who
advertise for clients, do not stipulate 'Mugs Only'.

All the large credit companies keep detailed dossiers
on all their clients. John Mort Green, for example,
would have a file started immediately he opened an
account. Every bet he makes is filed away after being
fed through a computer which produces a graph of
Green's betting methods and habits. The information
shows whether Green is a favourite backer or a
follower of one particular stable or jockey. This way
the bookmaker quickly discovers whether a client is
in the know about 'jobs' from a particular yard or
concerning one jockey. If a punter is using a system, it
will be uncovered and explained in full by the computer.
The file also is used to reveal the normal investment
of a punter. This is of tremendous value to the bookie.
If Green's usual stake is a 'fiver' and suddenly he
invests £50, it is obvious to the bookie that a horse has
been doing a bit of whispering in you know who's ear.

The bookmaker does not always terminate accounts
of punters who are obviously getting to know about
'jobs'. Often he uses these punters to his advantage.
If one of these clients goes on with a bet for a horse
hailing from the stable with which he is believed to
have connections, then the bookie knows he cannot
take any liberties with that runner. In other words, the

bookmaker has had his card marked. Likewise, if there is a horse in a race which one client is certain to know all about and the punter does not back it, then the bookmaker is safe to lay that runner.

It is possible to adapt this 'screening' system to beat the books. There is one famous jockey who will tell his friends to have 'as much as you like' on his mount. Many bookmakers have all jockeys and trainers followed to discover who are their friends and associates. As soon as a 'friend' of this particular jockey has a bet of, say, £200 the bookie says to himself, 'I know where this money has come from.' The jockey's 'real' cash, however, is going on another horse in the race, which will have 'taken a walk' in the market because of the deception.

British bookmakers seem to think the punter owes them a living. They scream and shout if a favourite wins the Derby as if we have lost the war or they are the victims of a second Great Train Robbery. They plead poverty, talk tearfully about their starving children at finishing school, and their crumbling twenty-room shack in Hampstead, before driving off in a new Jaguar for a seven-course sandwich at the Savoy Grill. The battle between the Tote and the bookmakers is not being won by either side, it is just being lost by the bookies. There is no question of the bookmakers being killed off by the Tote, they are committing suicide.

Basically, most of the bookmakers in the big-time are fair, but it is important that they should be seen to be honourable. In the past, many bookies have been gangsters. They were so crooked they were even able to double-cross death. This is why so many of them lived to such a stinking old age. Many businesses survived because the partners had long legs and little consciences. Some of today's bookies and their mates seem to be creating a deliberate parody of the past. They are not criminals. They would not harm a fly, not a poor one, anyway. So why do some of them go about their business so furtively, always looking guilty, talking from the side of the mouth and hiding their heads in elaborate coat collars? I am sure the answer is not that they are shy. These people, who are such an historic part of the British racing scene, should be endeavouring to improve their image, instead of fostering these sordid and suspect seeds. They cannot afford to allow any of these old seeds to germinate again. Bookmaking is a major industry in Britain. Enormous sums of money are handled every day.

Many of the men occupying the executive suites are real assets of society. They pump money back into racing. They donate to charity. Some have been known to go to church and nothing was missing from the collection afterwards. These same men should lead a campaign to clean up the industry and save it from the chop of the Tote monopolists. They must expose and dissociate themselves from the shady fringe element. They should call for a national charter, laying down a set of rules to be operated by every form of betting establishment in Britain. The industry must be seen to be respectable. This would do away with the intolerable situation of each 'shop' or organisation having its own rules. More important, it would chase out of town the 'Deliberate Deceivers', those petty thieves who proclaim, for instance, 'No Limit' and then say in small print, 'subject to rules'. Often a book of rules is not available. The rules, when you find them, show that the bookie is operating, in fact, the very opposite of a 'No Limit' system. The 'No Limit' sign is a deliberate deception in many cases.

There are also the bookmakers who change rules, or add to them, overnight, according to the luck of their clients the day before. It is not uncommon for a punter to go into a 'shop' to collect, say, £250 for a five-bob yankee to discover that a new notice has gone up on the wall overnight stating 'No client may win more than £100 on any one bet.' When he protests, 'That wasn't there yesterday,' the pirate in pin-stripes replies, 'I'm afraid you are mistaken, sir, that sign has been there for more than a year.' So old is the sign that if the irate punter is not careful he will get wet paint from the notice on his suit.

I am sincere about my concern for the bookmaking industry. Without bookmakers, I am derelict. I could not survive in a state where a Tote monopoly exists. I want all bookmakers to prosper . . . then so shall I.

Credit accounts are very convenient, providing you do not abuse them. Never entertain opening an account for more than you would be prepared to lose in cash each week. A bookmaker's account has the same basic dangers as any 'have now, pay later' scheme. There is more temptation to chase your losses when you are not using hard cash. Most people betting on a credit lose all sense of the value of money. So if you are not endowed with iron willpower, ignore all these induce-ments in advertisements in the national newspapers to apply for credit. You must keep proper books, listing every transaction, every penny invested, every penny won, and, most important, every penny lost. Do not cheat yourself. If you are not making racing pay, then be honest with yourself; after all, nobody else will be. I have said many harsh things about bookmakers, but really I am their friend. I cannot do without them, but they could well do without me. . . .

CHAPTER TEN

Reading a Race

Educationalists claim that the three 'R's' are the basis of learning. They should go back to school themselves. They cannot do simple addition. There are four 'R's', not three, as far as my idea of an education is concerned. The fourth 'R' stands for 'reading a race'. Any well-educated racegoer knows that race-reading is an essential part of any good punter's upbringing. How do you read a race? Let Professor Mort Green give you a crash course. After all, The Butterfly is one of the few people who could claim to have an honours degree in the punting profession.

Most punters fall in the trap of becoming too involved with the horse they have backed. Once your money is down, your thoughts should concentrate on where next week's bread is coming from. I have backed a horse to the tune of £500 and I have not known whether I had won or lost until five minutes after the finish of the race. I had to ask someone else the result because I had been captivated by the tussle for the fifth place. You can read all about the first three in tomorrow's morning newspapers.

As soon as the race starts, the professional punter must detach himself from any affiliation with one horse. He may have invested £1,000 but worry, shouting, nail-biting and any attempt at telepathy, will not improve the performance of his horse. The right attitude is for him to assume that he has lost his £1,000 and be looking to see how it is going to be retrieved another day. Remember, the majority of winners are horses that finished between fourth and eighth in their previous races. Therefore, if you ignore the leading group and concentrate on the middle division, you will be looking at the future winners.

Two-year-old races early in the season are ideal for spotting worthwhile future betting propositions. Watch for the youngster that is not in the betting, yet is always knocking on the door, but runs 'green' when the pressure is on in the last furlong. Next time you can rest assured that this same horse will know what it is all about. It was probably a non-trier on its first outing. When it makes a second appearance on the racecourse, keep an eye on the betting. If it is 6–1 or below, you should be on a 'knocking' each-way bet. Some stables use their second string jockey where a two-year-old has its first run. The star takes over when the animal is cherry ripe for winning. This way, the trainer covers himself in the event of the stewards holding an inquiry into any discrepancy in form or what might be regarded as abnormal improvement.

Often a two-year-old, in its first appearance on a racecourse in public, will be slow coming out of the starting stalls. This is because it is not sure what is expected of him. A two-year-old is a baby, and, as with humans, some mature and learn quicker than others. For a couple of furlongs the backward two-year-old will think he is still playing in a field, tossing his head sideways and trying to brush alongside his 'playmates'. It is the jockey's job to impress upon the youngster the serious nature of the business. If the youngster is slowly away, and then makes rapid headway, although never reaching the leaders, this is usually a good omen for the next occasion.

If you see a two-year-old running on strongly at the end of a five-furlong rush, check its breeding. You may discover that its pedigree suggests that the minimum trip is too short for the fellow. If that is the case, wait until it is entered over six or seven furlongs and then have a substantial wager. The trainer may have been just stupid. More likely, however, he was giving the animal a thorough grounding in competitive racing, without it having a chance of winning. A few 'coconuts' before its name would also ensure an appetising price when they were ready for it to 'go in'. Once again, the longer trip would be a handy excuse if the stewards asked any questions.

In the spring, look for two-year-olds that have matured early. The sort that win early in the season over the shortest distance are always compact, neat, muscular and often on the small side. Avoid long, leggy or big gross animals in the spring. They take longer to develop and come to hand much later in the year.

Some trainers deliberately run horses below or above their best distance in order to give the animal a pipe-opener and a test without exposing its true capabilities. So in distance races, make a note of any horse that sets a cracking pace for a mile and then blows up in the last four furlongs, and may even finish tailed off. A quick check on its breeding may well reveal that the horse obviously is a miler. Make a note of your discovery and wait until it turns out in a mile event or over a stiff seven furlongs, like at Newmarket, Sandown or Leicester. Likewise, you may observe something staying on in a mile and a half race as if it could go round again and climb Everest on the way. A scrutiny of the breeding in this case may well prove that it is likely to be a real true stayer and that one and a half miles was far too short for it to have been in with a chance. In this case, you would earmark this horse for a real test of stamina, such as a two mile or two and a quarter mile event.

Jockeys sometimes find themselves in all kinds of trouble in a race. Through no fault of their own, they may become boxed in and can do nothing except sit and wait for a clear passage. Often the corridor does not appear and a much-fancied runner bites the dust in dishonourable defeat, not even staging anything that could be mistaken for a challenge. The punters who have done their cash no doubt will bawl their heads off and bore other people with accusations against the jockey, and write off the animal as 'an old dog'. They could be right. If you are reading the race properly, you will know straight away if the animal is a 'dog'. However, if the horse was well-fancied in the market and genuinely had no chance because of being fenced in, then it is folly to discard it on to the scrap heap. You take my advice and give it another chance.

When a horse makes its run from way back, especially in a cavalry-charge sprint, with runners stretched in a line across the course, it is likely to meet with interference as it attempts to burst through. A small knock is enough to cause a horse distress and this will usually eclipse all hope of winning that day. A horse that was accelerating like a winner only to fall victim of an unfortunate incident in the scrimmaging, is worth supporting next time out. After all, on the following appearance it will be almost the equivalent of a winner without a penalty. However, any horse you notice swishing its tail when asked to produce something extra, is best forgotten. Consistent swishing of the tail is a firm indication that the horse does not enjoy the sport and would be better employed pulling a coal cart.

One day at Sandown I left the grandstand after the

third race so excited anyone would have thought that I
had been invited to dinner with the Duke of Norfolk,
or other old English gentry like 'Scobie' Breasley. As
I made my way out towards the unsaddling enclosure,
'Little John' stopped me and said, 'What the 'ell have
you got to look 'appy about? I thought you 'ad a
"monkey" on the favourite?'

'So I did,' I replied absent-mindedly.

'Well, you got dunne in the photo. You must be a
flaming masochist if that makes you laugh.'

'I was not watching what was happening to my
"monkey". I was more interested in studying the
beautiful creature that is going to bring me my next
fortune.'

'Little John' was right. I had lost in a photograph
finish, but I felt as if I had the only eight draws on a
football coupon.

The horse I had noted was Hasty Cloud. 'Hasty',
trained at Epsom by Harold Wallington, had been
beaten narrowly in the two previous Cambridgeshires.
That season it had less weight to carry in the autumn
handicap at Newmarket than it was forced to hump in
other years. All the so-called experts said 'Hasty' was
over the top, too old to win this competitive handicap.
I knew differently after that day at Sandown Park. Here
was an 'autumn' horse, an animal which reached its
peak towards the end of each season. I backed Hasty
Cloud at 100-8 from then on until the day of the
Cambridgeshire. 'Jock' Wilson was the jockey. Dep-
utising for the injured Duncan Keith, 'Jock' had the
race won before the 'bushes', despite Frankie Durr's
late rush on Eric Cousins-trained Commander-in-Chief.

The three 'R's' at school may help you to acquire a
wealth of knowledge. The fourth 'R' will put you on
the right track to acquiring a wealth of money.

Summary

The first important revelation I made in this book was that Coca Cola boxes are half an inch thicker than the Schweppes bitter lemon boxes; a worthwhile tip for Derby Day at Epsom when thousands of people are envious of giraffes as they strain their necks to see above some outrageous woman's hat blocking their view like an ugly skyscraper. Remember, too, my Ten Commandments. Here is a brief summary of them:

1. Never be greedy.
2. Never look at anything other than the best class horses, trainers and jockeys.
3. Forget those dreams of 100–1 winners and be content with horses in strong demand in the market.
4. Stop as soon as you are showing a profit on the day.
5. Back unpopular riders on the Tote.
6. Watch for eleventh-hour riding changes.
7. Follow money from big betting stables.
8. Learn to think the same way as trainers and jockeys.
9. Always get value by trying to beat the book.
10. Never lose confidence because you have lost everything else.

The law of libel prevents me from naming jockeys who would 'strangle' a horse for a fat back-hander from a bookmaker, but if you read between the lines of the newspaper commentaries and keep to my rules of reading a race, you should have no difficulty pinpointing the 'gutter' riders. Also leave alone those jockeys who are not overendowed with talent. I know that every jockey cannot be a Lester Piggott or 'Josh' Gifford, but that is their bad luck, do not make it yours!

Remember, too, that luck has no part in the professional punter's vocabulary. Luck is something people turn to when their ability is letting them down. If you are relying on luck to pull you through, then I advise you to reserve a bed at your local doss-house.

Forget forever coincidence bets. Just because an Irish-named horse once won on St. Crispin's Day, it does not follow that the coincidence will be an annual tradition.

Learn off by heart, so that you can recite quicker than your two-times table, all the details I listed of the premier jockeys, noting, in particular, on which courses they are most dangerous, and those who should be followed on the Tote. Pay attention to the information on the trainers, remembering the type of race and horse in which each one specialises.

The most important safety code you should bear in mind is, if you bet don't booze. Drinking on the racecourse is strictly for the birds – the cuckoos! And when you are on the racecourse, behave as if you are in your office, providing you work for a respectable concern! Keep away from the bars and you will save yourself from going behind them at Pentonville for debt.

When you are at the course, never back a horse until you have had a good look at it in the paddock and on the way down to the start. Watch especially for an elegant walker and a smooth mover, and avoid any horse that is sweating-up. Steer clear of any horse that is bandaged up as if it has been used as a war horse. Remember, though, an animal wearing blinkers for the first time often shows a marked improvement on its previous performances, so always take that into account when making your final calculations.

In the last hectic minute before the 'off' you must be stationed in that patch of land I have called No-Man's Land. There you will be able to follow the major market moves. Keep tailing the representatives who have the big money to invest. For much of the time they will be using sign language, like boy scouts in long trousers practising semaphore. At some point, though, they must resort to the English language, if it can be recognised as such. Make sure that you are there when the signals are translated into the name of a horse and the extent of the business. Keep on the move, keep looking, keep following, keep learning and, most important, keep yourself up to date with every development. Forget horses that are drawn badly and stick rigidly to the rule of only including well-bred horses and well-proven jockeys among your short-list. After a race, never discard your betting ticket until after the 'weigh-in'. You may not have noticed any offence, but the stewards might have spotted an infringement that could win you the race on an objection or an inquiry, but without your ticket you could just as well be trying to get money from a bank without having an account.

Make yourself familiar with all the jockeys' different riding styles so that you are able to read a race more easily than relying on colours and numbers. I do not want to bring politics into racing, but I cannot stress enough the need for any punter to be conservative. By all means be an extrovert in your social life, but when it comes to betting the modesty of a virgin is called for. Keep the pace slow and controlled, and always be in command of the situation. Resist panic measures at all costs. Once you have made your bet, you have passed the point of no return. Like the pilot, never make that move until you are sure of reaching your objective. Impose a strict limit on the amount that you are prepared to lose in any one day, week, month or year. Read the tips and articles on the racing pages of newspapers, but do not follow them blindly. If you back a loser, there must be only one person to blame – yourself.

Look out for late riding changes and try to read the trainer's mind to reveal the significance of the switch. It is better to be fully conversant with the form of all horses in one race than to have sketchy knowledge of runners throughout the whole meeting. Any 'springer' – a horse that shortens dramatically in the betting – often is worth support if you have no strong feelings about anything else in the race. Leave alone all races for amateur jockeys. They are riding for fun, but you should be backing for business. Those who are out for a day's play and those who are out for a day's pay are incongruous elements. Late money for horses trained by Ingham, Todd, Van Cutsem, Rohan, Frank Cundell, Sutcliffe Jnr. and W. Marshall is a powerful pointer and should never be ignored, even if not followed.

The professional punter must always ensure that he is getting value. Gambling on horses is all a question of buying and selling. The punter must be like the man on the Stock Exchange, knowing exactly when to strike a transaction to secure the best bargain. Avoid falling for a false 'springer'. There are many reasons for a phoney 'springer', but usually it is caused by a pile-up of money on a jockey's third leg of a treble after he has had two winners that day.

It does not matter whether you are going to the racecourse or the betting shop, arrive early. And like all conscientious students make sure that all your homework is complete by the beginning of each day. Be prepared to spend many days on the track or in the 'shop' without having a bet. Do not regard the time wasted. You should be preparing for future investments. The compulsive gambler is a cripple for life. He is sure to spend his life hobbling from betting shop to poor house.

Never hold post-mortems. As soon as the last race is over, all thoughts must turn to tomorrow. Maintain proper books showing how you fare each day and your financial position for the year. Every bet must be listed. Do not 'con' yourself by omitting the losers from your ledger. After all, you are fooling nobody but yourself. Included in your books should be all expenses, such as travelling fees and entrance charges to racecourses. You are making racing pay only if you are showing a balance over and above everything laid out in pursuit of the sport.

The professional punter must be capable of making decisions in a flash. This is no game for the ponderous or the hesitant. There is only time and money for one decision, and the first must be right.

Bear in mind what I told you about being a keen betting shop shopper. Always read *all* the rules and *all* the small print before considering using a 'shop' as your indoor racecourse for an afternoon's business. Do not be satisfied with signs that proclaim a 'No Limit', with the additional words 'subject to rules'. Find out exactly what their rules stipulate. If you can find a bookmaker who is operating a genuine and comprehensive no limit, so much the better.

To discover the winner, you must first sort out the losers. Once you have decided the horses which cannot possibly win, then you can concentrate on those that can. The safest races for the professional backer are stakes events for three- and two-year-olds, providing the fields are not too large. Forget all about 'sellers', unless something trained by Bill Marshall, Todd, Ingham or the young John Sutcliffe is backed as if being supported by The Dollar. Conditions races are also 'friends' of the punter. So always read the black print above the list of runners so that you know the qualifications for each race.

Never open a credit account with a bookmaker for more than you can afford to lose in any one week. When you are not actually laying out cash, money tends to lose its value. You may think that you are betting on the 'never never', but you will soon find it is really the 'ever ever'.

Any professional punter who is going to live long enough to retire to stud in the Bahamas or Majorca, must master the art of reading a race accurately. The first point to remember is shut out from your mind all thoughts of any horse that you have backed. Treat all the runners as equal as soon as they are 'off'. You must be prepared to put £1,000 on a horse and not be any more interested in that animal than any of the others. If you are not made in this ice-cold mould, admit it to yourself. You may not become one of racing's legendary winners, but neither will you be one of those sad, consistent, all-time losers. Try to assume that you have lost your money right from the start and be looking for a horse to retrieve your losses on another day. This way you will get racing in the right perspective. Money lost should be looked upon as only loaned. Most horses that win finished somewhere between fourth and the mid-division of their previous race. Therefore, the place to have your glasses trained in the last furlong is not on the leading group, but in that battle for fifth, sixth, seventh and eighth berths. Even if *your* horse is tanking along neck and neck to the line and victory will net you a cool £10,000, keep your eyes glued down the field. If your horse comes out worst in the photograph, you will need that one you have just noted as a potential winner. If you collect the £10,000, then you can read about that future winner you had marked from some sunny island.

Leave well alone leggy two-year-olds in the spring. Two-year-olds that win early in the year are compact, muscular and of the nippy variety, rather than generating colossal power. Look out for horses that have been running below or above their true distance and are reverted suddenly to the trip which suits them best. Finally, any horse continually swishing its tail is not a horse at all. It is a 'dog'.

Well, that is the end folks, which means for you it should be the beginning. I have taken care of every aspect of punting, except the kind of leisure stuff performed on the rivers, of course. Believe me, they are poles apart!

Index